GREAT TASTES

FRENCH

First published in 2010 by Bay Books, an imprint of Murdoch Books Pty Limited
This edition published in 2010.

Murdoch Books Australia
Pier 8/9
23 Hickson Road
Millers Point NSW 2000
Phone: +61 (0) 2 8220 2000
Fax: +61 (0) 2 8220 2558
www.murdochbooks.com.au

Murdoch Books UK Limited
Erico House, 6th Floor
93–99 Upper Richmond Road
Putney, London SW15 2TG
Phone: +44 (0) 20 8785 5995
Fax: +44 (0) 20 8785 5985
www.murdochbooks.co.uk

Chief Executive: Juliet Rogers
Publishing Director: Kay Scarlett
Publisher: Lynn Lewis
Senior Designer: Heather Menzies
Designer: Clare O'Loughlin
Production: Kita George
Index: Jo Rudd

ISBN: 9780681657922

PRINTED IN CHINA

IMPORTANT: Those who might be at risk from the effects of salmonella poisoning (the elderly, pregnant women, young children and those suffering from immune deficiency diseases) should consult their doctor with any concerns about eating raw eggs.

OVEN GUIDE: You may find cooking times vary depending on the oven you are using. For fan-forced ovens, as a general rule, set the oven temperature to 20°C (35°F) lower than indicated in the recipe.

GREAT TASTES
FRENCH

More than 120 easy recipes for every day

bay books

CONTENTS

FRENCH COOKING...6

STARTERS & LIGHT MEALS..............................8

MAINS...48

SALADS & SIDES..90

DESSERTS & BAKING....................................116

BASICS...146

INDEX...158

FRENCH COOKING

France's reputation for wonderful food and cooking is often thought of as being based on technical skills and extravagant, expensive ingredients. This is haute cuisine, 'classic cooking', which was developed by the chefs of the French aristocracy and reached its heyday in the nineteenth century. Nowadays, while this style of cooking is found mostly in expensive restaurants, many of the classic dishes are well within the capabilities of the adventurous home cook and are particularly suitable for special occasions and dinner parties. Many other more straightforward recipes can easily become part of the day-to-day repertoire. Importantly, sourcing good-quality seasonal ingredients is one of the main keys to success.

Fundamentally, French food is a regionally based cuisine and many French dishes are called after their place of origin, from entrecôte à la bordelaise, sole à la normande to boeuf à la bourguignonne. Eating your way around France, the regional differences are still very distinct, and most restaurants cook not only local dishes, but those of their own town or village. This is a result not only of tradition, but also of an enduring respect for local produce. Each area of France grows or produces food uniquely suited to its terrain and climate, from Bresse chickens to walnuts from Grenoble, butter from Normandy and mustard from Dijon. Nowadays, there is more crossover between the provinces, and in markets, the best, not just the local, vegetables can be found, but the notion of regional specialities still underlies French cooking.

This respect for ingredients extends also to only eating fruit and vegetables at the height of their season. Recipes change to reflect the best that each month has to offer, and every month, seasonal fruits and vegetables are eagerly awaited, from the summer melons of Provence to winter truffles in the Dordogne.

The French have also gone to great lengths to protect their ingredients and traditional methods of food preparation. The strict appellation d'origine contrôlée (AOC) system that they use to keep their cheese and wines as authentic as possible, is also being extended to an increasing number of other important and regionally based food products.

Despite the emergence of large supermarket chains around the nation, specialist food shops and weekly markets are an integral part of the French way of life.

The food of the north

Paris is a world culinary centre, where neighbourhood markets sell fantastic produce from all over France. Much of the city's reputation lies with its restaurants, a legacy of the revolution when private chefs were forced to find a new living. Parisians are legendarily discerning about their food and it is here you find the real home of the baguette, the country's most refined pâtisserie and finest cheese shops.

Brittany is a fishing and farming region with outstanding seafood, including native oysters and wonderful early fruits and vegetables. Sweet crêpes and savoury buckwheat galettes are found throughout the region. Its sea salt, sel de guerande, is used all over France.

Normandy's rich pasture is home to some of France's greatest cheeses: Camembert, Pont l'Evêque and Livarot; along with crème fraîche, butter and apples — three classic ingredients in French cuisine. There is also pré-salé lamb (lamb raised in salt marshes), mussels, oysters, cider and calvados.

Known as 'the Garden of France', the Loire Valley produces fruit, vegetables and white wines. Wild mushrooms are grown in the caves of Saumur. The region also produces fine goats' cheeses, including Crottin de Chavignol. Poitou-Charentes on the Atlantic Coast has some of France's best oyster beds near Marennes, and is home to Charentais melons, unsalted butter and Cognac.

Nord-Pas-de-Calais along the coast includes Boulogne-sur-mer, France's biggest fishing port. Inland are found the washed-rind Maroilles cheese, andouillettes and Flemish beers, used for cooking in dishes such as carbonnade à la flamande. Picardie has vegetables, fruit and pré-salé lamb.

Champagne-Ardennes is a rural region, with Champagne famous not just for its wine, but for cheeses such as Brie and Chaource. In the rugged north, the game forests of Ardennes have created a tradition of charcuterie (pork butchery). Jambon d'Ardennes and pâtés d'Ardennes are world-famous.

Bordering Germany, Alsace-Lorraine's mixed heritage is reflected in its cuisine. Its charcuterie is used in quiche lorraine, choucroute garnie, tarte flambée and baeckenoffe (stew). Meat dishes à la lorraine are served with red cabbage cooked in wine, while Alsace's baking has Germanic influences, with pretzels, rye bread and kugelhopf.

The food of the east and centre

Central France is made up of the regions of Auvergne and Limousin. With very cold winters, the cuisine of these areas tends to be hearty and potatoes and cabbages are heavily used for dishes such as aligot and potée auvergnate (one-pot pork and cabbage stew). Limousin is famous for its beef, lamb, pork and veal and Auvergne for its game and tiny green Puy lentils. The area also produces Cantal and Saint Nectaire cheeses, as well as blue cheeses such as Bleu d'Auvergne and Fourme d'Ambert. Auvergne is known for its bottled mineral waters, including Vichy and Volvic.

Burgundy is famous for its red and white wines with the wine industry centred around the town of Beaune. Burgundian dishes tend to be rich, full of flavour and a perfect match for the area's wines. Wine is also an important part of the region's cooking, and à la bourguignonne usually means cooked in red wine. Boeuf bourguignon, coq au vin, Bresse chicken cooked with cream and wild morels, snails filled with garlic herb butter and slices of jambon persillé (ham and parsley set in aspic) are all Burgundian classics. Dijon is synonymous with mustard and is also the home of pain d'épices (spicy gingerbread) and kir, made of white wine and crème de cassis from local blackcurrants.

One of France's great gastronomic capitals, Lyon is home to great restaurants, as well as many simple bouchons (traditionally working-class cafés) and brasseries, and is considered to be the charcuterie centre of France, Well-known dishes include salade lyonnaise, pike quenelles, poulet au vinaigre (chicken stewed in vinegar), potato gratins, the fresh herb cheese, cervelle de canut (silk weavers' brains) and pots (one pint bottles) of local Beaujolais or Côtes du Rhône. The surrounding countryside produces excellent fruit and vegetables, as well as AOC chickens from Bourg-en-Bresse.

The East of France rises up into the French Alps and is made up of three regions, Franche-Comté in the north and Savoie and Dauphiné in the south. These mountain regions have great cheesemaking traditions and in the summer, alpages cheeses such as Reblochon are still made from the milk from animals taken up to the high meadows. Beaufort and Comté are other mountain cheeses and dishes include fondues and raclettes. Potatoes are grown over the Centre and East, but it is Dauphiné that gives its name to the famous gratin dauphinois.

The food of the south and southwest

Bordeaux is associated with great wines and the grands crus of Médoc and Saint Emilion are world-famous, as are dessert wines from Sauternes. Red wine is used in cooking and these dishes are usually known as à la bordelaise, such as entrecôte à la bordelaise. Oysters from the Atlantic beds at Arcachon and pré-salé lamb from Pauillac are specialities.

Goose and duck confit and foie gras are the Dordogne and Lot's most famous exports along with the black truffles and walnuts of Périgord. Black truffles and foie gras are used as a garnish in many southwest dishes and these dishes are sometimes known as à la périgourdine. Walnuts are used in salade aux noix and in oils, and prunes are grown at Agen.

Gascony is a largely rural area that produces Armagnac and is famous, along with the Dordogne, for its foie gras, duck and goose confit, pâtés and terrines and for the use of goose fat in its cooking. Home-made and local specialities can be tasted at fermes auberges (farmhouse restaurants).

The southwest Basque country close to Spain flavours its food with spicy piment d'Espelette, dried chillies, which are also often used in the salting mixture for the local Bayonne ham. Tuna are caught off the Atlantic coast and the tradition of baking, such as making gâteau basque, is strong.

The flavours of Provence are those of the Mediterranean: olives, olive oil, garlic, aubergines, courgettes, tomatoes and herbes de Provence, along with melons from Cavaillon, strawberries and peaches. Provençal cuisine includes the strong flavours of aïoli, anchoïade and tapénade; pissaladière and pistou from the Italian-bordering Côte d' Azur; simple grilled fish and the classic bouillabaisse; red rice from the Camargue and honey and candied fruit.

Close to Spain, Languedoc-Roussillon is home to the famous Roquefort blue cheese, which is aged in caves. Along the coast, anchovies are conserved and the area uses salt cod in dishes such as brandade de morue. There is fresh seafood from the Mediterranean and bourride is Languedoc's bouillabaisse. Inland, there is hearty cassoulet from Carcassonne, Castelnaudary and Toulouse, sausages from Toulouse and pink garlic from Tarn.

Corsica, closer to Italy and Sardinia than France, has a tradition of Italian charcuterie, pasta and polenta. Stufato is a classic rich beef stew, where the sauce is served over pasta.

STARTERS & LIGHT MEALS

TAPENADE

SERVES 6

300 g (11 oz) black olives, pitted

3 tablespoons capers, rinsed

8 anchovies

1 garlic clove, crushed

180 ml (6 fl oz) olive oil

1 tablespoon lemon juice

2 teaspoons dijon mustard

1 teaspoon chopped thyme

1 tablespoon chopped parsley

1 Pound together the olives, capers, anchovies and garlic, either using a mortar and pestle or a food processor. Add the olive oil, lemon juice, mustard and herbs and pound or process again until you have a fairly rough paste.

2 Serve with bread or sliced raw vegetables for dipping. Tapenade can be kept, covered, in the fridge for several days.

AÏOLI

4 egg yolks

8 garlic cloves, crushed

½ teaspoon salt

2 tablespoons lemon juice

500 ml (17 fl oz/2 cups) olive oil

VEGETABLES, FOR DIPPING

6 baby carrots, trimmed with stalks left on

6 asparagus spears, trimmed and blanched

6 French beans, trimmed and blanched

6 button mushrooms, halved

1 yellow capsicum (pepper), seeded and cut into strips

1 red capsicum (pepper), seeded and cut into strips

6 small cauliflower florets

1 fennel bulb, cut into thin strips

1 Put the egg yolks, garlic, salt and half the lemon juice in a mortar and pestle or food processor and pound or mix until light and creamy.

2 Add oil, drop by drop at first from the tip of a teaspoon, whisking constantly until mixture begins to thicken. Add the remaining oil in a very thin, steady stream. (If you're using a processor, pour in the oil in a thin, steady stream with the motor running.) Season, add the remaining lemon juice and, if necessary, thin with a little warm water.

3 Arrange the vegetables around a large platter and serve the aïoli in a bowl in the centre. You can keep aïoli sealed in a sterilized jar in the fridge. It will last for up to 3 weeks.

CHICKEN LIVER PÂTÉ

SERVES 6

500 g (1 lb 4 oz) chicken livers

80 ml (3 fl oz/⅓ cup) brandy

90 g (3 oz) unsalted butter

1 onion, finely chopped

1 garlic clove, crushed

1 teaspoon chopped thyme

60 ml (2 fl oz/⅓ cup) thick (double/ heavy) cream

4 slices white bread

1 **Trim the chicken livers,** cutting away any discoloured bits and veins. Rinse them, pat dry with paper towels and then cut in half. Place in a small bowl with the brandy, cover and leave for a couple of hours. Drain the livers, reserving the brandy.

2 **Melt half the butter** in a frying pan, add the onion and garlic and cook over low heat until the onion is soft and has become transparent. Add the livers and thyme and stir over moderate heat until livers change colour. Add the reserved brandy and simmer for 2 minutes. Cool for 5 minutes.

3 **Place the livers and liquid** in a food processor and whiz until smooth. Add the remaining butter, chopped, and process again until smooth. (Or, roughly mash the livers with a fork, then push them through a sieve and mix with the melted butter.) Pour in the cream and process until just incorporated.

4 **Season the pâté** and spoon into an earthenware dish or terrine, smoothing the surface. Cover and refrigerate until firm. If the pâté is to be kept for more than a day, chill it and then pour cooled melted butter over the surface to seal.

5 **To make Melba toasts,** preheat the grill (broiler) and cut the crusts off the bread. Toast the bread on both sides, cut each piece into triangles and serve with the pâté.

TERRINE DE CAMPAGNE

SERVES 8

700 g (1 lb 9 oz) lean pork, cut into cubes

200 g (7 oz) pork belly, cut into strips

200 g (7 oz) chicken livers, trimmed

120 g (4 oz) bacon, chopped

1½ teaspoons sea salt

½ teaspoon black pepper

pinch of grated nutmeg

8 juniper berries, lightly crushed

3 tablespoons brandy

2 shallots, finely chopped

1 large egg, lightly beaten

sprig of bay leaves

8 thin slices bacon

1 Put the lean pork, pork belly, chicken livers and chopped bacon in a food processor and roughly chop into small dice (do this in two or three batches). Finely dice the meat.

2 Put the diced meat in a large bowl and add the sea salt, pepper, nutmeg, juniper berries and brandy. Mix carefully and leave to marinate in the fridge for at least 6 hours or overnight.

3 Preheat the oven to 180°C (350°F/Gas 4). Lightly butter a 20 x 7 x 9 cm (8 x 3 x 4 inch) terrine or loaf (bar) tin. Add the shallots and egg to the marinated meat and carefully combine.

4 Put a sprig of bay leaves in the base of the terrine and then line with the slices of bacon, leaving enough hanging over the sides to cover the top. Spoon filling into the terrine and fold the ends of the bacon over the top. Cover top with a layer of well-buttered baking paper and then wrap the whole terrine in a layer of foil.

5 Place the terrine in a large baking dish and pour water into the baking dish to come halfway up the sides of the terrine. Bake in this bain-marie for 1½ hours, or until the pâté is shrinking away from the sides of the terrine.

6 Lift the terrine out of the bain-marie and leave the pâté to cool, still wrapped in the paper and foil. Once cold, drain off the excess juices and refrigerate for up to a week. You may find that a little moisture has escaped from the pâté — this is quite normal and prevents it from drying out.

7 Run a knife around the inside of the terrine to loosen the pâté and then turn out onto a board and serve in slices.

ASPARAGUS WITH HOLLANDAISE SAUCE

SERVES 4

24 asparagus spears

HOLLANDAISE SAUCE
2 egg yolks
2 teaspoons lemon juice
90 g (3 oz) unsalted butter, cut into cubes

1 **Wash the asparagus** and remove the woody ends (hold each spear at both ends and bend it gently — it will snap at its natural breaking point). Cook the asparagus in a frying pan of simmering salted water for 4 minutes, or until just tender. Drain, then cool under cold running water.

2 **To make hollandaise sauce,** put the egg yolks and lemon juice in a saucepan over very low heat. Whisk continuously, adding the butter piece by piece until sauce thickens. Do not overheat or the eggs will scramble. Season. (Or, put the egg yolks, salt and pepper in a blender and process to combine. Heat the lemon juice and butter until boiling and then, with the motor running, pour the mixture onto the yolks in a thin, steady stream.)

3 **Arrange a few asparagus spears** on each plate and spoon the hollandaise sauce over the top.

ARTICHOKES VINAIGRETTE

SERVES 4

juice of 1 lemon
4 globe artichokes

VINAIGRETTE

5 tablespoons olive oil
2 spring onions (scallions), finely
    chopped
2 tablespoons white wine
2 tablespoons white wine vinegar
¼ teaspoon dijon mustard
pinch of sugar
1 tablespoon finely chopped parsley

1   **To prepare artichokes,** bring a large saucepan of salted water to the boil and add the lemon juice. Break the stalks from the artichokes, pulling out any strings at the same time, and then trim the bases flat. Add the artichokes to the water; put a small plate on top of them to keep them submerged. Simmer for 25–30 minutes, or until a leaf from the base can be pulled away easily. (The base will be tender when pierced with a skewer.) Cool quickly under cold running water, then drain upside down on a tray.

2   **To make the vinaigrette,** heat 1 tablespoon of oil in a small saucepan, add spring onion and cook over low heat for 2 minutes. Leave to cool a little, then add white wine, vinegar, mustard and sugar and gradually whisk in the remaining oil. Season well with salt and pepper. Stir in half the parsley.

3   **Place an artichoke** on each plate and gently prise it open a little. Spoon the dressing over the top, allowing it to drizzle into the artichoke and around the plate. Pour the remaining dressing into a small bowl for people to dip the leaves into. Sprinkle each artichoke with a little parsley.

4   **Eat the leaves one by one,** dipping them in vinaigrette and scraping the flesh off the leaves between your teeth. When you reach the middle, pull off any really small leaves and then use a teaspoon to remove the furry choke. Once you've got rid of the choke, you can eat the tender base or 'heart' of the artichoke.

FRENCH ONION SOUP

SERVES 6

50 g (2 oz) butter

750 g (1 lb 10 oz) onions, finely sliced

2 garlic cloves, finely chopped

45 g (1½ oz) plain (all-purpose) flour

2 litres (70 fl oz/8 cups) beef or chicken stock

250 ml (9 fl oz/1 cup) white wine

1 bay leaf

2 thyme sprigs

12 slices stale baguette

100 g (3½ oz) gruyère cheese, finely grated

1   Melt the butter in a heavy-based saucepan and add onion. Cook over low heat, stirring occasionally, for 25 minutes, or until onion is a deep golden brown and begins to caramelize.

2   Add garlic and flour and stir continuously for 2 minutes. Gradually blend in the stock and the wine, stirring all the time, and bring to the boil. Add the bay leaf and thyme and season. Cover the pan and simmer for 25 minutes. Remove the bay leaf and thyme and check the seasoning. Preheat the grill.

3   Toast the baguette slices, then divide among six warmed soup bowls and ladle the soup over the top. Sprinkle with the grated cheese and grill until the cheese melts and turns light golden brown. Serve immediately.

CHICKEN CONSOMMÉ

SERVES 4

STOCK

1 kg (2 lb 4 oz) chicken carcasses, chopped in half
185 g (7 oz) chicken legs
1 carrot, chopped
1 onion, chopped
1 celery stalk, chopped
2 parsley sprigs
20 black peppercorns
1 bay leaf
1 thyme sprig

CLARIFICATION MIXTURE

2 chicken drumsticks
1 carrot, finely chopped
1 leek, finely chopped
1 celery stalk, finely chopped
10 black peppercorns
1 parsley sprig, chopped
2 tomatoes, chopped
2 egg whites, lightly beaten
1 small carrot, cut into thin matchsticks
½ small leek, white part only, very finely shredded
sea salt

1 **To make the stock,** remove any skin and fat from the chicken carcasses and legs and place in a large heavy-based saucepan with 3 litres (105 fl oz/12 cups) cold water. Bring to the boil and skim off any fat that floats to the surface. Add the remaining ingredients and simmer for 1½ hours, skimming occasionally. Strain the stock (you should have about 1.5 litres (52 fl oz/6 cups)) and return to the clean saucepan.

2 **To make the clarification mixture,** remove the skin and meat from the chicken drumsticks and discard the skin. Chop the meat finely (you will need about 150 g/6 oz)) and mix with the carrot, leek, celery, peppercorns, parsley, tomato and egg white. Add 190 ml (6 fl oz/¾ cup) of the warm stock.

3 **Whisk clarification mixture** into strained stock. Simmer mixture for 1 hour or until stock is clear. As mixture simmers, the clarification ingredients will bind with any impurities and form a 'raft'. As the raft rises, gently move it with a wooden spoon to one side of the pan away from the main movement of the simmering stock (making it easier to ladle out later).

4 **Ladle out the chicken stock,** taking care not to disturb the raft, and strain through a fine sieve lined with damp muslin (cheesecloth). Place sheets of paper towel over the top of the consommé and quickly lift away to remove any remaining fat. Season with coarse sea salt (other salt will cloud the soup).

5 **Just before serving,** reheat the consommé. Place the carrot and leek in a saucepan of boiling water and cook for 2 minutes until just tender. Drain well, spoon into warmed soup bowls and pour the consommé over the top.

Note: While this is a labour-intensive recipe, this classic clear soup has a beautiful flavour that makes it worth the effort.

LEEK AND POTATO SOUP

SERVES 6

50 g (2 oz) butter

1 onion, finely chopped

3 leeks, white part only, sliced

1 celery stalk, finely chopped

1 garlic clove, finely chopped

200 g (7 oz) boiling potatoes, chopped

750 ml (27 fl oz/3 cups) chicken stock

220 ml (7 fl oz) cream

white pepper

2 tablespoons chives, snipped

1   Melt the butter in a large saucepan. Add the onion, leek, celery and garlic. Cover the pan and cook, stirring occasionally, over low heat for 15 minutes, or until vegetables are softened but not browned. Add potato and stock and bring to the boil.

2   Reduce heat. Leave to simmer, covered, for 20 minutes. Allow to cool a little before puréeing in a blender or food processor. Return to the clean saucepan.

3   Bring the soup gently back to the boil and stir in the cream. Season with salt and white pepper and gently reheat without boiling. Serve hot or, on a hot summer day, well chilled. Garnish with chives.

WATERCRESS SOUP

SERVES 4

30 g (1 oz) butter

1 onion, finely chopped

250 g (9 oz) boiling potatoes, diced

600 ml (21 fl oz/2½ cups) chicken stock

1 kg (2 lb 4 oz) watercress, trimmed and chopped

125 ml (4 fl oz/½ cup) pouring cream

125 ml (4 fl oz/½ cup) milk

freshly grated nutmeg

2 tablespoons chives, snipped

1 **Melt the butter** in a large saucepan and add the onion. Cover pan and cook over low heat until the onion is softened but not browned. Add potato and chicken stock and simmer for 12 minutes, or until the potato is tender. Add the watercress and cook for 1 minute.

2 **Remove from the heat** and leave the soup to cool a little before pouring into a blender or food processor. Blend until smooth and return to the clean saucepan.

3 **Bring the soup** gently back to the boil and stir in the cream and milk. Season with nutmeg, salt and pepper and reheat without boiling. Serve garnished with chives.

SOUPE AU PISTOU

SERVES 4

250 g (9 oz) dried haricot beans

2 teaspoons olive oil

1 onion, finely chopped

2 garlic cloves, crushed

1 celery stalk, chopped

3 carrots, diced

bouquet garni

4 all-purpose potatoes, diced

150 g (6 oz) small green beans, chopped

500 ml (17 fl oz/2 cups) chicken stock

3 tomatoes

4 zucchini (courgettes), diced

150 g (6 oz) vermicelli, broken into
  pieces

150 g (6 oz) peas, fresh or frozen

PISTOU

6 garlic cloves

4 large handfuls basil leaves

100 g (4 oz) parmesan cheese, grated

200 ml (7 fl oz) olive oil

1   Soak the beans in cold water overnight. Drain, put in a saucepan and cover with cold water. Bring to the boil, then lower heat and simmer for 1 hour, or until tender. Drain well.

2   To make the pistou, put the garlic, basil and parmesan in a food processor or a mortar and pestle and process or pound until finely chopped. Slowly add the olive oil, with the motor running if using the food processor, or pounding constantly with the mortar and pestle. Mix thoroughly. Cover with plastic wrap and set aside.

3   Heat the olive oil in a large saucepan, add the onion and garlic and cook over low heat for 5 minutes until softened but not browned. Add the celery, carrot and bouquet garni and cook for 10 minutes, stirring occasionally. Add the potato, green beans, chicken stock and 1.75 litres (60 fl oz) water and simmer for 10 minutes

.

4   Score a cross in the top of each tomato. Plunge them into boiling water for 20 seconds, then drain and peel the skin away from the cross. Chop tomatoes finely, discarding the cores. Add to the soup with the zucchini, haricot beans, vermicelli and peas, and cook for 10 minutes or until tender (if you are using frozen peas, add them at the last minute just to heat through). Season and serve with pistou on top.

Note: Basil is more usually associated with Italy than France but, in fact, the herb originated not in Italy, but in India. It was introduced to Europe in the sixteenth century. It is often used in Southern French cooking as a perfect match for Provençal tomatoes and olive oil. It can be bought in pots or as bunches. Better still, try growing your own in summer.

CAULIFLOWER SOUP

SERVES 4

30 g (1 oz) butter
1 onion, finely chopped
1 small celery stalk, finely chopped
600 g (1 lb 5 oz) cauliflower, broken into florets
440 ml (15 fl oz) chicken stock
315 ml (11 fl oz/1¼ cups) milk
1 bay leaf
1 thyme sprig
125 ml(4 fl oz/½ cup) pouring cream
freshly grated nutmeg
2 tablespoons chives, snipped

1 Melt the butter in a large saucepan and add the onion and celery. Cook over low heat until vegetables are softened but not browned. Add the cauliflower, stock, milk, bay leaf and thyme and bring to the boil. Cover the pan, reduce the heat and simmer for 20 minutes, or until the cauliflower is tender.

2 Leave soup to cool, then remove the bay leaf and thyme. Purée the soup in a blender or food processor until smooth and return to the clean saucepan. Bring to the boil, stirring constantly, add cream and reheat just at a simmer (do not boil). Season with salt, white pepper and nutmeg, then serve sprinkled with chives.

GARLIC SOUP

SERVES 4

2 heads of garlic (about 30 cloves in all), cloves separated

150 ml (5 fl oz) olive oil

125 g (5 oz) bacon, finely chopped

1 large potato, diced

1.5 litres (52 fl oz/6 cups) chicken stock or water

bouquet garni

3 egg yolks

CHEESE CROUTONS

½ baguette or 1 ficelle, sliced

50 g (2 oz) gruyère cheese, grated

1 Smash the garlic with the flat side of a knife and peel. Heat 1 tablespoon of the oil in a large heavy-based saucepan and cook the bacon over moderate heat for 5 minutes without browning. Add the garlic and potato and cook for 5 minutes until softened. Add the stock and bouquet garni, bring to the boil and simmer for 30 minutes, or until the potato starts to dissolve into the soup.

2 Put the egg yolks in a large bowl and pour in remaining oil in a thin stream, whisking until thickened. Gradually whisk in the hot soup. Strain back into the saucepan, pressing to extract all the liquid, and heat gently without boiling. Season.

3 To make the cheese croutons, preheat grill (broiler) and lightly toast the bread on both sides. Sprinkle with cheese and grill until melted. Place a few croutons in each warm bowl and ladle the soup over the top, or serve the croutons on the side.

CABBAGE SOUP

SERVES 4

100 g (4 oz) dried haricot beans

125 g (5 oz) bacon, cubed

40 g (1½ oz) butter

1 carrot, sliced

1 onion, chopped

1 leek, white part only, roughly chopped

1 turnip, peeled and chopped

bouquet garni

1.25 litres (44 fl oz/5 cups) chicken stock

400 g (14 oz) white cabbage, finely shredded

white pepper

1 **Soak the beans overnight in cold water.** Drain, put in a saucepan and cover with cold water. Bring to the boil and simmer for 5 minutes, then drain. Put the bacon in the same saucepan, cover with water and simmer for 5 minutes. Drain and pat dry with kitchen paper.

2 **Melt the butter** in a large, heavy-based saucepan, add the bacon and cook for 5 minutes, without browning. Add beans, carrot, onion, leek and turnip and cook for about 5 minutes. Add the bouquet garni and chicken stock and bring to the boil. Cover and simmer for 30 minutes. Add cabbage, uncover and simmer for 30 minutes, or until beans are tender. Remove the bouquet garni before serving and season to taste.

PETITS FARCIS

SERVES 4

2 small zucchini (courgettes), halved lengthways

4 tomatoes

2 small red capsicum (peppers), halved lengthways and seeded

4 tablespoons olive oil

2 red onions, chopped

2 garlic cloves, crushed

250 g (9 oz) minced (ground) pork

250 g (9 oz) minced (ground) veal

50 g (2 oz) tomato purèe

80 ml (2½ fl oz/⅓ cup) white wine

2 tablespoons chopped parsley

50 g (2 oz) parmesan cheese, grated

80 g (3 oz) fresh breadcrumbs

1   Preheat oven to 180°C (350°F/Gas 4). Grease a large roasting tin with oil. Hollow out centres of the zucchini with a spoon, leaving a border round the edge. Chop flesh finely.

2   Cut the tops from the tomatoes (don't throw away the tops). Use a spoon to hollow out the centres, catching the juice in a bowl, and chop the flesh roughly. Arrange the vegetables, including the red capsicum, in the roasting tin. Brush the edges of the zucchini with a little of the oil. Pour 125 ml (4 fl oz/½ cup) water into the roasting tin.

3   Heat half the oil in a large frying pan. Cook onion and garlic for 3 minutes, or until softened. Add the mince and stir for 5 minutes until the meat browns, breaking up any lumps with the back of a fork. Add the chopped zucchini and cook for a further 3 minutes. Add the tomato pulp and juice, tomato purèe and wine. Cook, stirring occasionally, for 10 minutes.

4   Remove frying pan from the heat and stir in the parsley, parmesan cheese and breadcrumbs. Season well with salt and pepper. Spoon the mixture into the vegetables. Place the tops back on the tomatoes. Sprinkle vegetables with the remaining oil and bake for 45 minutes, or until the vegetables are tender.

PROVENÇAL TART

SERVES 6

2 tablespoons olive oil
1 large white onion, finely chopped
10 tomatoes (or 2 x 400 g tins chopped tomatoes)
1 teaspoon tomato purée
2 garlic cloves, finely chopped
1 tablespoon roughly chopped oregano, plus a few whole leaves to garnish
1 red capsicum (pepper), halved lengthways and seeded
1 yellow capsicum (pepper), halved lengthways and seeded
6 anchovies, halved
12 pitted olives
drizzle of olive oil

PASTRY

250 g (9 oz) plain (all-purpose) flour
150 g (6 oz) butter, diced
1 egg yolk, beaten

1 To make the pastry, sift the flour into a bowl, add butter and rub in with your fingertips until the mixture resembles breadcrumbs. Add the egg yolk and a little cold water (about 2–3 teaspoons) and mix with the blade of a palette knife until the dough just starts to come together. Shape dough into a ball with your hands. Wrap in plastic wrap and refrigerate for at least 30 minutes.

2 Heat the oil in a frying pan, add the onion. Cook over a very low heat, covered, for 20 minutes, stirring often, until softened but not browned.

3 Score a cross in the top of each tomato. Plunge into boiling water for 20 seconds. Drain and peel skin away from cross. Chop tomatoes, discarding cores. Add tomato, tomato purée, garlic and oregano to the pan. Simmer for 20 minutes, stirring occasionally until mixture is a paste. Leave to cool.

4 Roll out pastry to fit a 34 x 26 cm (14 x 11 inch) shallow baking tray. Prick the pastry gently all over (do not pierce right through). Cover with clingfilm and chill for 30 minutes. Preheat the oven to 200°C (400°F/Gas 6) and preheat the grill.

5 Place capsicums, skin side up, under hot grill (broiler) until skin is black and blistered. Cool, peel away skin. Slice capsicums thinly.

6 Line pastry shell with a crumpled piece of greaseproof paper and fill with baking beads (use dried beans or rice if you don't have beads). Blind bake the pastry for 10 minutes, remove paper and beads and bake for a further 3–5 minutes, or until the pastry is just cooked but still very pale. Reduce the oven to 180°C (350°F/Gas 4).

7 Spread tomato over pastry, add capsicum, anchovies and olives. Brush with oil; bake for 25 minutes. Top with oregano.

PISSALADIÈRE

SERVES 6

40 g (1½ oz) butter

1 tablespoon olive oil

1.5 kg (3 lb 5 oz) onions, thinly sliced

2 tablespoons thyme leaves

1 tablespoon olive oil

16 anchovies, halved lengthways

24 pitted olives

BREAD DOUGH

2 teaspoons dried yeast

120 ml (4 fl oz/½ cup) warm water

250 g (9 oz) plain (all-purpose) flour

½ teaspoon salt

3 tablespoons olive oil

1 **To make the bread dough,** mix the yeast with the warm water. Leave for 10 minutes in a warm place until frothy.

2 **Sift flour into a large bowl.** Add salt, olive oil and yeast mixture. Mix until the dough clumps together and forms a ball. Turn out onto a lightly floured work surface. Knead, adding a little more flour or warm water, if needed, to make a soft dough that's dry to the touch. Knead 10 minutes, until smooth, and an impression made by a finger springs back at once.

3 **Rub the inside of a large bowl with olive oil.** Roll the ball of dough around in the bowl to coat it with oil, then cut a shallow cross on the top of the ball. Cover the bowl with a tea towel or put in a plastic bag and leave in a draught-free spot for 1–1½ hours or until the dough has doubled in size.

4 **Knock back the dough** by punching it several times to expel the air and then knead it again for a couple of minutes.

(At this stage the dough can be stored in the fridge for 4 hours, or frozen. Bring back to room temperature before continuing.) Leave in a warm place until doubled in size.

5 **Melt the butter with the olive oil** in a saucepan and add the onion and half the thyme. Cover the saucepan and cook over low heat for 45 minutes, stirring occasionally, until the onion is softened but not browned. Season and cool. Preheat the oven to 200°C (400°F/Gas 6).

6 **Roll out bread dough** to roughly fit an oiled 34 x 26 cm (13½ x 10½ inch) shallow baking tray. Brush with the olive oil, then spread with the onion.

7 **Lay the anchovies in a lattice pattern** and arrange the olives in the lattice diamonds. Bake for 20 minutes, until the dough is lightly browned. Sprinkle with the remaining thyme.

TARTE FLAMBÉE

SERVES 6

2 tablespoons olive oil

2 white onions, sliced

100 g (4 oz) cream cheese

185 ml (6 fl oz/¾ cup) fromage frais or other low-fat curd cheese

200 g (7 oz) piece of bacon, cut into lardons

1 quantity bread dough (page 149)

1 **Preheat the oven to 230°C** (450°F/Gas 8). Heat olive oil in a saucepan and fry the onion until softened but not browned. Beat the cream or curd cheese with the fromage frais and then add the onion and bacon and season well.

2 **Roll out the bread dough** into a rectangle — the dough needs to be quite thin, like a pizza — and place on an oiled baking tray. Fold the edge of the dough over to make a slight rim. Spread the topping over the dough, right up to the rim, and bake for 10–15 minutes, or until the dough is crisp and cooked and the topping browned. Cut into squares to serve.

HAM, MUSHROOM AND CHEESE CRÊPES

SERVES 6

1 quantity crêpe batter (page 154)

20 g (1 oz) butter

150 g (6 oz) mushrooms, sliced

2 tablespoons pouring cream

150 g (6 oz) gruyère cheese, grated

100 g (4 oz) ham, chopped

1   Heat a large crêpe or frying pan and grease with a little butter or oil. Pour in enough batter to coat the base of the pan in a thin, even layer and tip out any excess. Cook over moderate heat for about a minute, or until the crêpe starts to come away from the side of the pan. Turn the crêpe and cook on the other side for 1 minute or until lightly golden. Stack the crêpes on a plate, with pieces of greaseproof paper between them, and cover with clingfilm while you cook the rest of the batter to make six large crêpes.

2   Preheat the oven to 180°C (350°F/Gas 4). Heat butter in a frying pan, add the mushrooms, season well and cook, stirring, for 5 minutes, or until all the liquid from the mushrooms has evaporated. Stir in the cream, cheese and ham.

3   Lay one crêpe on a board or work surface. Top with about a sixth of the filling and fold the crêpe into quarters. Place it on a baking tray and then fill and fold the remaining crêpes. Bake for 5 minutes and then serve immediately.

OMELETTE AUX FINES HERBES

SERVES 4

15 g (½ oz) butter

2 spring onions (scallions), finely chopped

1 garlic clove, crushed

2 tablespoons chopped parsley

2 tablespoons chopped basil

½ tablespoon chopped tarragon

2 tablespoons thick (double/heavy) cream

8 eggs, lightly beaten

oil

1 Melt the butter in a frying pan and cook the shallots and garlic over low heat until tender. Stir in the herbs and tip into a bowl. Allow to cool. Mix in the cream and eggs; season well.

2 Heat a little oil in a non-stick frying pan. Pour a quarter of the batter into the pan and cook gently, constantly pulling the set egg around the edge of the pan into the centre, until the omelette is set and browned underneath and the top is just cooked. Fold omelette into three. Slide it out of the pan onto a plate with the seam underneath. Serve hot, for someone else to eat while you cook the remaining three omelettes.

ZUCCHINI OMELETTE

SERVES 4

80 g (3 oz) butter

400 g (14 oz) zucchini (courgettes), sliced

1 tablespoon basil, finely chopped

pinch of ground nutmeg

8 eggs, lightly beaten

1 **Melt half the butter** in a non-stick 23 cm (9 inch) frying pan. Add the zucchini and cook over moderate heat for about 8 minutes, until lightly golden. Stir in the basil and nutmeg, season with salt and pepper; ook for 30 seconds. Transfer to a bowl and keep warm.

2 **Wipe out the pan,** return it to the heat and melt the remaining butter. Lightly season the eggs and pour into the pan. Stir gently over high heat. Stop stirring when the mixture begins to set in uniform, fluffy small clumps. Reduce the heat and lift the edges with a fork to prevent it catching. Shake the pan from side to side to prevent the omelette sticking. When it is almost set but still runny on the surface, spread the zucchini down the centre. Using a spatula, fold the omelette over and slide onto a serving plate.

CROQUE MONSIEUR

80 g (3 oz) unsalted butter

20 g (1 oz) plain (all-purpose) flour

185 ml (6 fl oz/¾ cup) milk

½ teaspoon dijon mustard

1 egg yolk

grated nutmeg

12 slices white bread

6 slices ham

125 g (5 oz) gruyère cheese, grated

1   Melt 20 g (1 oz) of the butter in a saucepan, add the flour and stir over low heat for 3 minutes. Slowly add the milk and mustard, whisking constantly. Leave to simmer until the mixture has thickened and reduced by about a third. Remove from the heat and stir in the egg yolk. Season with salt, pepper and nutmeg and leave to cool completely.

2   Place half the bread slices on a baking tray. Top each piece of bread with a slice of ham, then with some of the sauce, then gruyère cheese and finally with another piece of bread. Melt half the remaining butter in a large frying pan and fry the sandwiches on both sides until they are golden brown, adding remaining butter when you need it. Cut each sandwich in half to serve.

PIPERADE

SERVES 4

2 tablespoons olive oil

1 large onion, thinly sliced

2 red capsicums (peppers), seeded and cut into batons

2 garlic cloves, crushed

750 g (1 lb 10 oz) tomatoes

pinch of cayenne pepper

8 eggs, lightly beaten

10 g (½ oz) butter

4 thin slices of good-quality ham

1 Heat the oil in a large heavy-based frying pan and cook the onion for 3 minutes, or until it has softened. Add the pepper and garlic, cover and cook for 8 minutes to soften — stir frequently and don't allow it to brown.

2 Score a cross in the top of each tomato. Plunge them into boiling water for 20 seconds, then drain and peel the skin away from the cross. Chop the tomatoes, discarding the cores. Spoon the chopped tomato and cayenne over the pepper, cover the pan and cook for a further 5 minutes.

3 Uncover the pan and increase the heat. Cook 3 minutes or until the juices have evaporated, shaking the pan often. Season well with salt and pepper. Add the eggs and scramble into the mixture until they are cooked.

4 Heat the butter in a small frying pan and fry the ham. Arrange on the piperade and serve at once.

ONION TART

SERVES 6

1 quantity tart pastry (page 150)
50 g (2 oz) butter
550 g (1 lb 4 oz) onions, finely sliced
2 teaspoons fresh thyme leaves
3 eggs
275 ml (9 fl oz/1 cup) thick (double/ heavy) cream
60 g (2 oz) gruyère cheese , grated
grated nutmeg

1 Preheat the oven to 180°C (350°F/Gas 4). Line a 23 cm (9 in) fluted loose-based tart tin with the pastry. Line the pastry shell with a crumpled piece of baking paper and baking beads (use dried beans or rice if you don't have beads). Blind bake the pastry for 10 minutes, remove the paper and beads and bake for a further 3–5 minutes, or until the pastry is just cooked but still very pale.

2 Meanwhile, melt the butter in a small frying pan and cook the onion, stirring, for 10–15 minutes or until tender and lightly browned. Add the thyme leaves and stir well. Leave to cool. Whisk together the eggs and cream and add the cheese. Season with salt, pepper and nutmeg.

3 Spread the onion into the pastry shell and pour the egg mixture over the top. Bake for 35–40 minutes, or until golden brown. Leave in the tin for 5 minutes before serving.

FLAMICHE

SERVES 6

1 quantity tart pastry (page 150)

500 g (1 lb 2 oz) leeks, white part only, finely sliced

50 g (2 oz) butter

180 g (7 oz) Maroilles (soft cheese), Livarot or Port-Salut, chopped, or other firm, full-flavoured cheese

1 egg

1 egg yolk

60 ml (2 fl oz/¼ cup) thick (double/ heavy) cream

1 egg, lightly beaten

1 **Preheat the oven to 180°C** (350°F/Gas 4) and put a baking tray on the top shelf. Use three-quarters of the pastry to line a 23-cm (9 inch) , or fluted loose-based tart tin.

2 **Cook leek for 10 minutes** in boiling salted water, then drain. Heat the butter in a frying pan, add the leek and cook, stirring, for 5 minutes. Stir in the cheese. Tip into a bowl and add the egg, egg yolk and cream. Season and mix well.

3 **Pour filling into pastry shell** and smooth. Roll out the remaining pastry to cover the pie. Pinch the edges together and trim. Cut a hole in the centre and brush egg over the top. Bake for 35–40 minutes on the baking tray until browned. Leave in the tin for 5 minutes before serving.

QUICHE LORRAINE

SERVES 8

1 quantity tart pastry (page 150)

25 g (1 oz) butter

300 g (11 oz) bacon, diced

250 ml (9 fl oz/1 cup) thick (double/ heavy) cream

3 eggs

grated nutmeg

1 **Preheat the oven to 200°C** (400°F/Gas 6). Line a 25 cm (10 inch) fluted loose-based tart tin with the pastry. Line the pastry shell with a crumpled piece of greaseproof paper and baking beads (use dried beans or rice if you don't have beads). Blind bake the pastry for 10 minutes, remove the paper and beads and bake for a further 3–5 minutes, or until the pastry is just cooked but still very pale. Reduce the oven to 180°C (350°F/Gas 4).

2 **Melt the butter** in a small frying pan and cook the bacon until golden. Drain on paper towels.

3 **Combine cream and eggs** and season with salt, pepper and nutmeg. Scatter the bacon into the pastry shell and then pour in the egg mixture. Bake for 30 minutes, or until filling is set. Leave in the tin for 5 minutes before serving.

ASPARAGUS AND ARTICHOKE QUICHE

SERVES 4–6

PASTRY

220 g (7¾ oz/1¾ cups) plain (all-purpose) flour

100 g (3½ oz) chopped chilled butter

2 tablespoons iced water

FILLING

150 g (5½ oz) asparagus spears, woody ends trimmed, and cut into bite-sized pieces

3 eggs

125 ml (4 fl oz/½ cup) pouring cream

40 g (1½ oz/⅓ cup) grated gruyère cheese

140 g (5 oz) marinated artichoke hearts, quartered

60 g (2 oz/½ cup) grated cheddar cheese

1 **To make the pastry,** sift flour into a bowl. Using your fingertips, rub in the butter until the mixture resembles fine breadcrumbs. Make a well in the centre and add iced water. Mix with a flat-bladed knife, using a cutting action, until the mixture comes together in beads. Add a little more water if the dough is too dry. Turn out onto a lightly floured work surface and gather into a ball. Cover with plastic wrap and refrigerate for 20 minutes.

2 **Preheat the oven** to 190°C (375°F/Gas 5). Roll out the pastry between two sheets of baking paper to fit a shallow loose-based 25 cm (10 inch) flan (tart) tin. Lift the pastry into the tin and press it well into the sides. Trim off any excess by rolling a rolling pin across the top of the tin. Refrigerate pastry for 20 minutes. Cover the shell with baking paper, fill evenly with baking beads or uncooked rice and bake for 15 minutes,

or until the pastry is dried out and golden. Remove the paper and beads and cool slightly. Reduce the oven temperature to 180°C (350°F/Gas 4).

3 **To make the filling,** blanch the asparagus in a saucepan of boiling salted water. Drain, then refresh in ice-cold water. Lightly beat together the eggs, cream and gruyère cheese, then season. Spread artichoke hearts over the cooled pastry, along with the asparagus. Pour on the egg and cream mixture and sprinkle with the cheddar cheese. Bake for 25 minutes, or until the filling is set and golden. Cover with foil if the pastry becomes too brown before the filling is fully set.

ROCKET, BASIL AND LEEK QUICHE

SERVES 4–6

150 g (5½ oz) rocket (arugula), stalks removed

185 g (6½ oz/1½ cups) plain (all-purpose) flour

125 g (4½ oz) butter, chopped

1–2 tablespoons iced water

1 tablespoon oil

1 large leek, white part only, thinly sliced

2 garlic cloves, crushed

2 eggs

125 ml (4 fl oz/½ cup) milk

125 ml (4 fl oz/½ cup) pouring cream

basil leaves, to garnish

parmesan cheese shavings, to garnish (optional)

1 Preheat oven to 210°C (415°F/Gas 6–7). Wash the rocket and shake off the excess water. Finely slice the leaves.

2 Sift flour into a bowl. Using your fingertips, rub in the butter until mixture resembles fine breadcrumbs. Add the iced water and mix to a soft dough with a flat-bladed knife, using a cutting action. Turn onto a lightly floured work surface and knead for 10 seconds, or until smooth. Refrigerate, covered in plastic wrap, for 30 minutes.

3 Roll out the pastry, between two sheets of plastic wrap, large enough to cover the base and side of a shallow 23 cm (9 inch) flan (tart) tin. Cover with a sheet of baking paper and spread baking beads or uncooked rice over it. Bake 10 minutes, remove the paper and beads, then bake for 5 minutes or until lightly golden. Reduce the heat to 180°C (350°F/Gas 4).

4 Heat the oil in a frying pan, add the leek and garlic and stir over low heat for 5 minutes or until the leek is soft. Add the rocket and stir over heat for 1 minute. Remove from the heat; allow to cool. Spread over the base of the pastry shell. Combine the eggs, milk and cream and whisk until smooth. Pour into the pastry shell. Bake for 50 minutes, or until set and golden. Serve topped with basil leaves and shaved parmesan.

VOL-AU-VENTS

MAKES 4

250 g (9 oz) block ready-made puff pastry, thawed

1 egg, lightly beaten

SAUCE AND FILLING

40 g (1½ oz) butter

2 spring onions (scallions), finely chopped

2 tablespoons plain (all-purpose) flour

375 ml (13 fl oz/1½ cups) milk

your choice of filling (see Note)

1 **Preheat the oven to** 220°C (425°F/Gas 7). Line a baking tray with baking paper. Roll out the pastry to a 20 cm (8 inch) square. Cut four circles with a 10 cm (4 inch) cutter. Place the rounds onto the tray and cut 6 cm (2½ inch) circles into the centre of the rounds with a cutter, taking care not to cut right through. Place the tray in the refrigerator for 15 minutes.

2 **Using a floured knife blade,** 'knock up' the sides of each pastry round by making even indentations 1 cm (½ inch) apart around the circumference. This should allow even rising of the pastry as it cooks. The dough can be made ahead of time up to this stage and frozen until needed.

3 **Carefully brush** the pastry with the egg, avoiding the 'knocked up' edge as any glaze spilt on the sides will stop the pastry from rising. Bake for 15–20 minutes, or until the pastry has risen and is golden brown and crisp. Cool on a wire rack.

Remove the centre from each pastry circle and discard any partially cooked pastry from the centre. The pastry can be returned to the oven for 2 minutes to dry out if the centre is undercooked. The pastry cases are now ready to be filled.

4 **To make the sauce,** melt the butter in a saucepan, add the spring onion and stir over low heat for 2 minutes, or until soft. Add the flour and stir for 2 minutes, or until lightly golden. Gradually add the milk, stirring until smooth. Stir constantly over medium heat for 4 minutes, or until the mixture boils and thickens. Season well. Remove and stir in your choice of filling.

Note: Add 350 g (12 oz) of any of the following to your white sauce: sliced, cooked mushrooms; cooked prawns (shrimp); chopped, cooked chicken breast; poached, flaked salmon; cooked and dressed crabmeat; oysters; steamed asparagus.

RATATOUILLE TARTS

MAKES 12

PASTRY

375 g (13 oz/3 cups) plain (all-purpose) flour

175 g (6 oz) chilled butter, chopped

125 ml (4 fl oz/½ cup) iced water

FILLING

1 eggplant (aubergine) (about 500 g/ 1 lb 2 oz)

60 ml (2 fl oz/¼ cup) oil

1 onion, chopped

2 garlic cloves, crushed

2 zucchini (courgettes), sliced

1 red capsicum (pepper), seeded, membrane removed and chopped

1 green capsicum (pepper), seeded, membrane removed and chopped

250 g (9 oz) cherry tomatoes, halved

1 tablespoon balsamic vinegar

125 g (4½ oz/1 cup) grated cheddar cheese

---

1 Sift flour into a bowl. Using your fingertips, rub in the butter until the mixture resembles fine breadcrumbs. Make a well in the centre and add the iced water. Mix with a flat-bladed knife until the dough just comes together. Add more water, if needed. Gather into a ball; divide into 12 portions.

2 Grease 12 loose-based fluted flan (tart) tins measuring 8 cm (3¼ inches) across the base and 3 cm (1¼ inches) deep. Roll each portion of dough out on a sheet of baking paper to a circle a little larger than the tins. Lift into tins, press into the sides, then trim away excess pastry. Refrigerate for 30 minutes.

3 Preheat oven to 200°C (400°F/Gas 6). Place tins on baking trays, prick pastry all over with a fork. Bake 20–25 minutes, or until pastry is fully cooked and lightly golden. Cool completely.

4 To make filling, cut eggplant into 2 cm (¾ inch) cubes, put into a colander and sprinkle with salt. After 20 minutes, rinse, drain and pat dry.

5 Heat 2 tablespoons of oil in a large frying pan. Cook eggplant in batches for 8–10 minutes each, or until browned; add more oil, if needed. Drain on paper towels. Heat remaining oil, add the onion and cook over medium heat for 5 minutes, or until very soft. Add garlic and cook for 1 minute, then add the zucchini and capsicum and cook, stirring frequently, for 10 minutes, or until softened. Add the eggplant and tomatoes. Cook, stirring, for 2 minutes. Transfer to a bowl, stir in vinegar, then cover and cool completely.

6 Reduce oven to 180°C (350°F/Gas 4). Divide the mixture evenly among pastry shells with a slotted spoon; drain off any excess liquid. Sprinkle with cheddar. Cook for 10–15 minutes.

TOURTE DE BLETTES

SERVES 6–8

60 g (2 oz/½ cup) sultanas (golden raisins)

2 tablespoons brandy

400 g (14 oz) plain (all-purpose) flour

100 g (4 oz) icing (confectioners') sugar

250 g (9 oz) unsalted butter, softened and chopped

3 eggs

800 g (1 lb 12 oz) silverbeet (Swiss chard), stalks removed

100 g (4 oz/⅔ cup) pine nuts, toasted

3 green cooking apples, peeled, cored and thinly sliced

1 teaspoon grated lemon zest

115 g (4 oz) mild goat's cheese

1 egg yolk, to glaze

icing (confectioners') sugar, extra, to dust

1   Soak the sultanas in the brandy.

2   To make the pastry, sift the flour and 1 tablespoon of the icing sugar into a large bowl. Using your fingertips, rub in the butter until the mixture resembles fine breadcrumbs. Make a well in the centre, add one egg and mix with a flat-bladed knife, using a cutting action, until the mixture comes together in beads. Add 1 tablespoon water if mixture is too dry. Gather together and lift onto a lightly floured work surface. Press into a ball and flatten to a disc. Wrap in plastic wrap and refrigerate for 30 minutes.

3   Preheat oven to 180°C (350°F/Gas 4). Heat a baking tray in the oven.

4   Wash silverbeet and pat dry. Place in a food processor with the two remaining eggs and the remaining icing sugar. Process to chop silverbeet and combine; don't overprocess.

Transfer to a bowl. Drain the sultanas and add to the bowl with the pine nuts, then season.

5   Bring the pastry to room temperature, then break into two portions. Roll one half and use to line a 26 cm (10½ inch) loose-based flan (tart) tin.

6   Peel the apples, slice thinly and toss with the lemon zest. Put the silverbeet mixture on the pastry and top with the crumbled goat's cheese. Spiral the apple slices on top.

7   Roll out remaining pastry and cover the pie. Trim off the excess pastry and seal edges with a little water. Crimp edges.

8   Brush pie with egg yolk. Bake for about 45 minutes, or until golden. Cool slightly, then dust with icing sugar. Serve warm or cold.

GOAT'S CHEESE GALETTE

SERVES 6

PASTRY
125 g (4 oz/1 cup) plain (all-purpose) flour

60 ml (2 fl oz/¼ cup) olive oil

3–4 tablespoons chilled water

FILLING
1 tablespoon olive oil

2 onions, thinly sliced

1 teaspoon thyme leaves

125 g (4 oz) ricotta

100 g (3½ oz) goat's cheese

2 tablespoons pitted Niçoise olives

1 egg, lightly beaten

60 ml (2 fl oz/¼ cup) cream

1 **For the pastry,** sift the flour and a pinch of salt into a large bowl and make a well. Add the olive oil and mix with a flat-bladed knife until crumbly. Gradually add the water until the mixture comes together. Remove and pat together to form a disc. Refrigerate for 30 minutes.

2 **For the filling,** heat the olive oil in a frying pan. Add the onion, cover and cook over low heat for 30 minutes. Season and stir in half the thyme. Cool slightly.

3 **Preheat oven to 180° C** (350°F/Gas 4). Lightly flour the work bench and roll out the pastry to a 30 cm (12 inch) circle. Spread onion evenly over the pastry leaving a 2 cm (¾ inch) border. Sprinkle the ricotta and the goat's cheese evenly over the onion. Place olives over the cheeses, then sprinkle with the remaining thyme. Fold the pastry border into the edge of the filling, gently pleating as you go.

4 **Combine egg and cream** in a small bowl, then carefully pour over the filling. Bake on a heated baking tray on the lower half of the oven for 45 minutes, or until the pastry is golden. Serve warm or at room temperature.

PAN BAGNAT

SERVES 4

4 crusty bread rolls, or 1 French
    baguette sliced into 4 chunks

1 garlic clove

60 ml (2 fl oz/¼ cup) olive oil

1 tablespoon red wine vinegar

3 tablespoons fresh basil leaves, torn

2 tomatoes, sliced

2 hard-boiled eggs, sliced

75 g (2½ oz) tin tuna

8 anchovy fillets

1 small cucumber, sliced.

½ green capsicum (pepper), thinly sliced

1 French shallot, thinly sliced

1 Slice the bread rolls in half and remove some of the soft centre from the tops. Cut the garlic clove in half and rub the insides of the rolls with the cut sides. Sprinkle both sides of the bread with olive oil, vinegar, salt and pepper.

2 Place all the salad ingredients on the base of the rolls, cover with the other half and wrap each sandwich in foil. Press firmly with a light weight and stand in a cool place for 1 hour before serving.

BEEF AND RED WINE PIES

MAKES 6

60 ml (2 fl oz/¼ cup) oil

1.5 kg (3 lb 5 oz) chuck steak, cubed

2 onions, chopped

1 garlic clove, crushed

30 g (1 oz/¼ cup) plain (all-purpose) flour

310 ml (10¾ fl oz/1¼ cups) good-quality dry red wine

500 ml (17 fl oz/2 cups) beef stock

2 bay leaves

2 thyme sprigs

2 carrots, chopped

500 g (1 lb 2 oz) shortcrust (pie) pastry

500 g (1 lb 2 oz) block ready-made puff pastry, thawed

1 egg, lightly beaten

1 **Grease 6 metal pie tins** measuring 9 cm (3½ inches) along the base and 3 cm (1¼ inches) deep.

2 **Heat 2 tablespoons of the oil** in a large frying pan and brown the steak in batches. Remove from pan. Heat remaining oil in the pan, add onion and garlic and stir over medium heat until golden brown. Add flour and stir for 2 minutes, or until well browned. Remove heat. Gradually stir in wine and stock.

3 **Return to the heat and stir** until the mixture boils and thickens. Return the meat to the pan, add the bay leaves and thyme and simmer for 1 hour. Add the carrot and simmer for another 45 minutes, or until the sauce has thickened. Season, then remove the bay leaves and thyme. Allow to cool.

4 **Preheat oven to 200°C** (400°F/Gas 6). Divide shortcrust pastry into six portions and roll out each one between two sheets of baking paper to a 25 cm (10 inch) square, 3 mm

(⅛ inch) thick. Cut a circle from each piece of pastry big enough to line the base and side of each pie tin. Place in tins and trim the edges. Line each pastry shell with baking paper and fill with baking beads or uncooked rice. Place on a baking tray and bake for 8 minutes. Remove paper and beads. Bake a further 8 minutes, or until pastry is lightly browned. Let cool.

5 **Divide the puff pastry** into six portions and roll each one between two sheets of baking paper to a square. Cut circles from the squares of dough, to fit the tops of the pie tins. Divide filling evenly among the pastry cases and brush the edges with some of the beaten egg. Cover with a puff pastry round and trim any excess pastry, pressing the edges with a fork to seal. Cut a slit in the top of each pie. Brush pie tops with remaining beaten egg and bake for 20–25 minutes, or until the pastry is cooked and golden brown.

ZUCCHINI SOUFFLÉ

SERVES 4

15 g (½ oz) butter, melted

1½ tablespoons dried breadcrumbs

350 g (12 oz) zucchini (courgettes),
  chopped

125 ml (4 fl oz/½ cup) milk

30 g (1 oz) butter

30 g (1 oz) plain flour

75 g (3 oz) gruyère or parmesan cheese,
  finely grated

3 spring onions (scallions), finely
  chopped

4 eggs, separated

1 Brush a 1.5 litre soufflé dish with the melted butter and then tip the breadcrumbs into the dish. Rotate the dish to coat the side completely with breadcrumbs. Tip out the excess.

2 Cook the zucchini in boiling water for 8 minutes, until tender. Drain and then put the zucchini in a food processor with the milk and mix until smooth. Alternatively, mash the zucchini with the milk and then press it through a sieve with a wooden spoon. Preheat the oven to 180°C (350°F/Gas 4).

3 Melt the butter in a heavy-based saucepan. Stir in the flour to make a roux. Cook, stirring, for 2 minutes over a low heat; do not let the roux brown. Remove from heat and add zucchini purée, stirring until smooth. Return to the heat; bring to the boil. Simmer, stirring, for 3 minutes. Remove from heat, pour into a bowl, add cheese and spring onion and season well. Mix until smooth, beat in egg yolks until smooth again.

4 Whisk the egg whites in a clean dry bowl until they form soft peaks. Spoon a quarter of the egg white onto the soufflé mixture and quickly but lightly fold it in, to loosen the mixture. Lightly fold in remaining egg white. Pour into the soufflé dish and run your thumb around the inside rim of the dish, about 2 cm (1 inch) into the soufflé mixture (try not to wipe off the butter and breadcrumbs). This ridge helps the soufflé to rise without sticking.

5 Bake for 45 minutes, or until the soufflé is well risen and wobbles slightly when tapped. Test with a skewer through a crack in the side of the soufflé — the skewer should come out clean or slightly moist. If the skewer is slightly moist, by the time the soufflé makes it to the table it will be cooked in the centre. Serve immediately.

BLUE CHEESE SOUFFLÉ

SERVES 4

15 g (½ oz) butter, melted
30 g (1 oz) butter
30 g (1 oz) plain flour
250 ml (1 cup) milk
125 g (5 oz) blue cheese, mashed
4 egg yolks
grated nutmeg
5 egg whites

1   Preheat the oven to 200°C (400°F/Gas 6). Cut a strip of baking paper long enough to fold around a 1.25 litre (42 fl oz/ 5 cup) soufflé dish, then fold in half and tie around the dish so it sticks 2–3 cm (1 inch) above the top. Brush the inside of the dish and the collar with the melted butter and place the dish on a baking tray.

2   Melt the butter in a heavy-based saucepan and stir in the flour to make a roux. Cook, stirring, for 2 minutes over a low heat without allowing the roux to brown. Remove from heat and add milk gradually, stirring after each addition until smooth. Return to the heat; bring to the boil. Simmer, stirring, for 3 minutes, then remove from the heat.

3   Stir the cheese into the sauce until it melts (it might separate but keep stirring — it will correct itself). Beat in the yolks, one at a time, beating well after each addition. Season with nutmeg, salt and pepper and pour into a large bowl.

4   Whisk the egg whites in a clean dry bowl until they form soft peaks. Spoon a quarter of the egg white onto the soufflé mixture and quickly but lightly fold it in, to loosen the mixture. Lightly fold in remaining egg white. Pour into the soufflé dish.

5   Bake the soufflé for 20–25 minutes, or until it is well risen and wobbles slightly when tapped. Test with a skewer through a crack in the side of the soufflé — the skewer should come out clean or slightly moist. If the skewer is slightly moist, by the time the soufflé makes it to the table it will be cooked in the centre. Serve immediately.

GARLIC PRAWNS

SERVES 4

24 large prawns (shrimp)

6 garlic cloves, crushed

1–2 small red chillies, very finely chopped

250 ml (9 fl oz/1 cup) olive oil

60 g (2 oz) butter

2 tablespoons chopped parsley

1 Peel and devein the prawns, leaving the tails intact. Preheat the oven to 220°C (425°F/Gas 7). Sprinkle the garlic and chilli into four cast iron or gratin dishes. Divide the oil and butter among the dishes.

2 Put the dishes on a baking tray in the oven and heat for about 6 minutes, or until the butter has melted.

3 Divide prawns among the dishes (put them in carefully, without splashing yourself with hot oil) and bake for about 7 minutes, or until the prawns are pink and tender. Sprinkle with parsley and serve immediately with crusty bread.

SCALLOPS PROVENCALE

SERVES 4 AS A STARTER

600 g (1 lb 4 oz) ripe tomatoes

3 tablespoons olive oil

1 onion, finely chopped

4 French shallots, finely chopped

60 ml (2 fl oz/¼ cup) dry white wine

60 g (2 oz) butter

20 fresh scallops, cleaned and dried, with shells

4 garlic cloves, crushed

2 tablespoons finely chopped parsley

½ teaspoon thyme leaves

2 tablespoons fresh breadcrumbs

1 **Score a cross in the** base of each tomato. Place the tomatoes in boiling water for 20 seconds, then plunge into cold water and peel. Cut each tomato in half and scoop out the seeds with a teaspoon and discard them. Finely dice the tomato flesh.

2 **Heat 2 tablespoons** of oil in a frying pan over medium heat until hot. Add the onion and shallots, then reduce the heat to low and cook slowly for 5 minutes, or until soft. Add the wine and simmer for several minutes until reduced slightly, then add the tomato. Season with salt and pepper and cook, stirring occasionally, for 20 minutes, or until thick and pulpy. Preheat the oven to moderate 180°F (350°F/Gas 4).

3 **Heat the butter and remaining oil** in a frying pan over high heat until foamy. Cook half the scallops for 1–2 minutes each side, or until lightly golden and cooked to your liking. Remove and repeat with the remaining scallops. Set aside.

4 **Add the garlic** to the hot scallop pan and stir for 1 minute. Remove from heat; stir in the parsley, thyme and breadcrumbs.

5 **Warm the shells** on a baking tray in the oven. Place a small amount of tomato mixture on each shell, top with a scallop and sprinkle with breadcrumb and parsley mixture.

Note: If the shells are not available, simply serve the scallops on a small plate. Place them on a bed of the tomato mixture and top with the breadcrumb mixture.

MAINS

BOEUF A LA FICELLE

SERVES 4

1 x 800 g (1 lb 12 oz) centre-cut beef fillet

900 ml (31 fl oz) beef stock

1 swede (rutabaga), cut into batons

1 carrot, cut into batons

1 celery stalk, cut into batons

2 potatoes, cut into chunks

¼ cabbage, chopped

4 spring onions (scallions), trimmed into long lengths

1 bay leaf

2 thyme sprigs

a few parsley sprigs

1 Trim the beef of any fat and sinew and cut into four even pieces. Tie each piece of beef around its circumference with kitchen string so it keeps its compact shape. Leave a long length of string attached to lower the beef in and out of the stock.

2 Place the stock in a saucepan, bring to the boil and add the vegetables and herbs. Cook over moderate heat for about 8 minutes, or until the vegetables are tender. Lift out the vegetables with a slotted spoon and keep warm. Discard the herbs and skim the stock of any fat or foam that floats to the surface.

3 Season the beef with salt, then lower into the simmering stock, keeping the strings tied around the saucepan handle or a wooden spoon balanced over the pan. Cook for about 6 minutes for rare, or 10 minutes for medium-rare, depending on your tastes.

4 Place each piece of beef in a large shallow bowl and loop the end of the string onto the rim of the bowl. Add the cooked vegetables and ladle some of the cooking broth over the top to serve.

CHICKEN WITH FORTY CLOVES OF GARLIC

SERVES 4

2 celery stalks, including leaves

2 rosemary sprigs

4 thyme sprigs

4 flat-leaf (Italian) parsley sprigs

1 x 1.6 kg (3 lb 8 oz) chicken

40 garlic cloves, unpeeled

2 tablespoons olive oil

1 carrot, roughly chopped

1 small onion, cut into 4 wedges

250 ml (9 fl oz/1 cup) white wine

1 baguette, cut into slices

small herb sprigs, to garnish

1 Preheat the oven to 200°C (400°F/Gas 6). Put a chopped celery stalk and 2 sprigs each of the rosemary, thyme and parsley into the chicken cavity. Add 6 cloves of garlic. Tie the legs together and tuck the wing tips under.

2 Brush the chicken liberally with some of the oil and season well. Scatter about 10 more garlic cloves over the base of a large casserole dish. Put remaining sprigs of herbs, chopped celery, carrot and onion in the casserole.

3 Put the chicken in the dish. Scatter the remaining garlic cloves around the chicken and add the remaining oil and the wine. Cover and bake for 1 hour 20 minutes, or until the chicken is tender and the juices run clear when the thigh is pierced with a skewer.

4 Carefully lift the chicken out of the casserole dish and strain off the juices into a small saucepan. Use tongs to pick out the garlic cloves from the strained mixture. Spoon off the fat from the juices and boil for 2–3 minutes to reduce and thicken a little.

5 Cut chicken into serving portions, pour over a little of the juices and scatter with the garlic. Toast the baguette slices, then garnish the chicken with herb sprigs and serve with the bread to be spread with the soft flesh squeezed from the garlic.

COQ AU VIN

SERVES 8

2 x 1.6 kg (3 lb 8 oz) whole chicken

750 ml (26 fl oz/3 cups) red wine

2 bay leaves

2 sprigs thyme

250 g (9 oz) bacon slices, diced

60 g (2 oz) butter

20 baby onions

250 g (9 oz) button mushrooms

1 teaspoon oil

30 g (1 oz) plain (all-purpose) flour

1 litre (35 fl oz/4 cups) chicken stock

125 ml (4 fl oz/½ cup) brandy

2 teaspoons tomato paste
    (concentrated purée)

30 g (1 oz), softened butter

1 tablespoon plain (all-purpose) flour

2 tablespoons chopped flat-leaf (Italian)
    parsley

1   **Joint each chicken** into eight pieces by removing both legs and cutting between the joint of the drumstick and the thigh. Cut down either side of the backbone and lift it out. Turn chicken over and cut through the cartilage down the centre of the breastbone. Cut each breast in half, leaving the wing attached to the top half.

2   **Put wine,** bay leaves, thyme, salt and pepper in a bowl with the chicken. Cover. Refrigerate for 4 hours, or overnight.

3   **Blanch the bacon** in boiling water, then drain, pat dry and sauté in a frying pan until golden. Remove. Melt 15 g (½ oz) of the butter in the pan, add the onions and sauté until browned. Lift out and set aside.

4   **Melt a further 15 g (½ oz)** of the butter, add mushrooms, season with salt and pepper and sauté for 5 minutes. Remove and set aside.

5   **Drain the chicken,** reserving the marinade, and pat the chicken dry. Season. Add remaining butter and the oil to the frying pan, add chicken and sauté until golden. Stir in the flour.

6   **Transfer the chicken** to a large saucepan or casserole and add the stock. Pour the brandy into the frying pan and boil, stirring, for 30 seconds to deglaze the pan. Pour over the chicken. Add the marinade, onions, mushrooms, bacon and tomato paste. Cook over medium heat for 45 minutes, or until the chicken is cooked through.

7   **If the sauce** needs thickening, lift out the chicken and vegetables and bring the sauce to the boil. Combine the butter and flour and whisk into the sauce. Boil, stirring, for 2 minutes or until thickened. Add the parsley and return the chicken and vegetables to the sauce.

CHICKEN CHASSEUR

SERVES 4

1 x 1.6 kg (3 lb 8 oz) chicken

1 tablespoon oil

60 g (2 oz) butter

2 shallots, finely chopped

125 g (5 oz) button mushrooms, sliced

1 tablespoon plain (all-purpose) flour

125 ml (4 fl oz/½ cup) white wine

2 tablespoons brandy

2 teaspoons tomato purée

220 ml (7½ fl oz) chicken stock

2 teaspoons chopped tarragon

1 teaspoon chopped parsley

CROUTONS

2 slices bread

olive oil

1   Joint the chicken into eight pieces by removing both legs and cutting between the joint of the drumstick and the thigh. Cut down either side of the backbone and lift it out. Turn the chicken over and cut through the cartilage down the centre of the breastbone. Cut each breast in half, leaving the wing attached to the top half.

2   Heat the oil in a frying pan or saucepan and add half the butter. When the foaming subsides, add the chicken and sauté in batches on both sides until browned. Lift out onto a plate and keep warm. Pour the excess fat out of the pan.

3   Melt remaining butter in the pan, add shallot and cook gently until softened but not browned. Add mushrooms and cook, covered, over moderate heat for 3 minutes.

4   Add the flour and cook, stirring constantly, for 1 minute. Stir in the white wine, brandy, tomato purée and stock. Bring to the boil, stirring constantly, then reduce the heat and add the tarragon. Season.

5   Return the chicken to the pan, cover and simmer for 30 minutes, or until the chicken is tender and cooked through. Sprinkle with parsley to serve.

6   To make the croutons, trim the crusts from the bread and cut the bread into moon shapes with a biscuit cutter. Heat the olive oil in a frying pan and fry the bread until golden. Drain the croutons on paper towels and serve hot with the chicken.

PORK CHOPS WITH BRAISED RED CABBAGE

SERVES 4

BRAISED RED CABBAGE

30 g (1 oz) clarified butter

1 onion, finely chopped

1 garlic clove, crushed

1 small red cabbage, shredded

1 dessert apple, peeled, cored and finely sliced

75 ml (2¼ fl oz) red wine

1 tablespoon red wine vinegar

¼ teaspoon ground cloves

1 tablespoon sage, finely chopped

15 g (½ oz) clarified butter

4 x 200 g (7 oz) pork chops, trimmed

75 ml (2½ fl oz) white wine

400 ml (12 fl oz) chicken stock

3 tablespoons double (thick/heavy) cream

1½ tablespoons dijon mustard

4 sage leaves

1   **To braise the cabbage,** put the clarified butter in a large saucepan, add the onion and garlic and cook until softened but not browned. Add cabbage, apple, wine, vinegar, cloves and sage and season with salt and pepper. Cover the pan and cook for 30 minutes over very low heat. Uncover the pan and cook, stirring, for a further 5 minutes to evaporate any liquid.

2   **Heat the clarified butter** in a frying pan, season the chops and brown well on both sides. Add the wine and stock, cover and simmer for 20 minutes, or until the pork is tender.

3   **Remove the chops** from the frying pan and strain the liquid. Return the liquid to the pan, bring to the boil and cook until reduced by two-thirds. Add the cream and mustard and stir over very low heat ,without allowing the mixture to boil, until the sauce has thickened slightly. Pour over the pork chops and garnish with sage. Serve with the red cabbage.

SERVES 4

1½ tablespoons tarragon, chopped

1 garlic clove, crushed

50 g (1¾ oz) butter, softened

1.6 kg (3 lb 8 oz) whole chicken

2 teaspoons oil

150 ml (5 fl oz) chicken stock

1½ tablespoons white wine

1 tablespoon plain (all-purpose) flour

1 tablespoon tarragon leaves

150 ml (5 fl oz) thick (double/heavy) cream

1 Preheat the oven to 200°C (400°F/Gas 6). Combine the chopped tarragon, garlic and half the butter. Season with salt and pepper and place inside the cavity of the chicken. Tie the legs together and tuck the wing tips under.

2 Heat remaining butter with the oil in a large flameproof casserole dish over low heat and brown the chicken on all sides. Add chicken stock and wine. Cover the casserole and bake in the oven for 1 hour 20 minutes, or until the chicken is tender and the juices run clear when a thigh is pierced with a skewer. Remove the chicken, draining all the juices back into the casserole dish. Cover with foil and a tea towel (dish towel) and allow to rest.

3 Skim a tablespoon of the surface fat from the cooking liquid and put it in a small bowl. Skim the remainder of the fat from the surface and discard. Add the flour to the reserved fat and mix until smooth. Whisk quickly into the cooking liquid and stir over medium heat until the sauce boils and thickens.

4 Strain the sauce into a clean saucepan and add tarragon leaves. Simmer for 2 minutes, stir in the cream, then reheat without boiling. Season with salt and pepper. Carve the chicken and spoon the sauce over the top to serve.

GRILLED RED MULLET WITH HERB SAUCE

SERVES 4

4 x 200 g (7 oz) red mullet
3 tablespoons lemon juice
3 tablespoons olive oil

HERB SAUCE
100 g (3½ oz) spinach leaves
3 tablespoons olive oil
1 tablespoon white wine vinegar
1 tablespoon chopped parsley
1 tablespoon chopped chives
1 tablespoon chopped chervil
1 tablespoon finely chopped capers
2 anchovy fillets, finely chopped
1 hard-boiled egg, finely chopped

1 **Preheat a griddle or barbecue.** Make a couple of deep slashes in the thickest part of each fish. Pat the fish dry and sprinkle inside and out with salt and pepper. Drizzle with a little lemon juice and olive oil and cook on the griddle or barbecue for 4–5 minutes each side, or until the fish flakes when tested with the tip of a knife. Baste with the lemon juice and oil during cooking.

2 **To make the sauce,** wash spinach and put it in a large saucepan with just the water clinging to the leaves. Cover the pan and steam the spinach for 2 minutes, or until just wilted. Drain, cool and squeeze with your hands to get rid of the excess liquid. Finely chop. Mix with the oil, vinegar, herbs, capers, anchovy and egg in a food processor or pestle and mortar. Spoon sauce onto a plate and place the fish on top.

ROAST CHICKEN

SERVES 4

45 g (1½ oz) butter, softened

1 x 1.6 kg (3 lb 8 oz) chicken

1 tarragon or rosemary sprig

315 ml (11 fl oz/1¼ cups) chicken stock

1 **Preheat the oven** to 200°C (400°F/Gas 6). Place half the butter inside the chicken with the tarragon or rosemary. Rub chicken with the remaining butter and season. Tie the legs together and tuck the wing tips under. Put, breast side down, in a roasting tin and add the stock.

2 **Cover chicken** loosely with foil and roast for 30 minutes, basting occasionally. Uncover, turn the chicken and roast for 30–40 minutes, or until golden brown and juices run clear when the thigh is pierced with a skewer.

3 **Remove the chicken** from the tin, cover with foil and a tea towel and leave to rest. Put the tin on the stove top and skim off most of the fat. Boil rapidly until the juices reduce and become syrupy. Strain and serve with the chicken.

RACK OF LAMB WITH HERB CRUST

SERVES 4

2 x 6-chop racks of lamb, trimmed and bones cleaned (ask your butcher to do this)

1 tablespoon oil

80 g (3 oz/1 cup) fresh breadcrumbs

3 garlic cloves

3 tablespoons flat-leaf (Italian) parsley, finely chopped

½ tablespoon thyme leaves

½ teaspoon finely grated lemon zest

60 g (2 oz) butter, softened

250 ml (9 fl oz/1 cup) beef stock

1 garlic clove, extra, finely chopped

1 sprig thyme

1 Preheat the oven to 250°C (500°F/Gas 10). Score the fat on racks in a diamond pattern. Rub the rack with a little of the oil and season with salt and pepper.

2 Heat the oil in a frying pan over high heat, add the lamb and brown for 4–5 minutes. Remove and set aside. Do not wash the pan as you will need it later.

3 In a large bowl, mix breadcrumbs, garlic, parsley, thyme and lemon rind. Season, then mix in the butter to form a paste.

4 Firmly press a layer of breadcrumb mixture over the fat on the racks, leaving the bones and base clean. Bake in a baking dish for 12 minutes for medium-rare. Rest the lamb while you make the jus.

5 To make a jus, add the beef stock, extra garlic and thyme sprig to the roasting pan juices, scraping the pan. Return this liquid to the original frying pan and simmer over high heat for 5–8 minutes, until sauce is reduced. Strain; serve on the side.

BRAISED SAUSAGES WITH PUY LENTILS

SERVES 4

1 tablespoon olive oil

100 g (4 oz) pancetta, cut into cubes

2 red onions, finely chopped

12 Toulouse sausages, or any good-quality fresh pork sausages

2 garlic cloves, bruised

2 thyme sprigs

300 g (11 oz/1½ cups) Puy lentils or tiny blue-green lentils

750 ml (26 fl oz/3 cups) tinned chicken consommé

150 g (6 oz) baby English spinach leaves, finely chopped

crusty bread, to serve

1 **Heat the olive oil** in a large heavy-based frying pan, add the pancetta and sauté over medium–high heat for about 5 minutes, or until browned. Using a slotted spoon, remove the pancetta and place in a bowl.

2 **Add the onion to the pan** and sauté over medium heat for 5–6 minutes, or until softened and only lightly browned. Remove the onion and add to the pancetta.

3 **Fry the sausages** in the same pan, in batches, if necessary, for 10 minutes, or until deep golden all over, turning often.

4 **Return the pancetta** and onion to the pan, add the garlic, thyme and lentils and stir together well. Pour in the consommé and bring to the boil. Reduce the heat, cover and simmer for 30–35 minutes, or until the lentils are tender.

5 **Stir in the spinach** and season to taste with sea salt and freshly ground black pepper. Serve in warmed bowls with crusty bread.

BAKED TROUT WITH FENNEL AND CAPERS

SERVES 4

2 fennel bulbs, with fronds

1 leek, white part only, thickly sliced

1 large carrot, cut into batons

2 tablespoons olive oil

2 tablespoons capers, rinsed and patted dry

1 shallot, finely chopped

1 x 1.3 kg (3 lb) brown or rainbow trout, or 4 x 300 g (11 oz) trout, gutted and fins removed

1 or 2 bay leaves

25 g (1 oz) butter, cut into 4 cubes

4 slices lemon

200 ml (7 fl oz) fish stock

50 ml (1½ fl oz) dry vermouth

2 tablespoons pouring (whipping) cream

2 tablespoons chopped chervil

1 Preheat the oven to 200°C (400°F/Gas 6). Cut off the fronds from the fennel bulbs and finely chop them. Thinly slice bulbs and place in a roasting tin with the leek and carrot. Drizzle a tablespoon of olive oil over vegetables, add salt and pepper and then toss well to coat them in the oil and seasoning. Bake on the middle shelf of the oven for 20 minutes.

2 Mix chopped fennel fronds with the capers and shallot. Season the inside of the trout and fill with the fennel and caper stuffing. Put the bay leaf, cubes of butter and the lemon slices inside the fish, too. Combine the fish stock and vermouth.

3 Remove the vegetables from the oven, stir well and reduce the oven temperature to 140°C (275°F/Gas 1). Lay the trout over the vegetables and pour the stock and vermouth over the fish. Season the trout and drizzle with the remaining tablespoon of olive oil. Cover the top of the tin with foil and return to the oven for 1 hour 15 minutes or until the fish is cooked through. The flesh should feel flaky through the skin and the inside will look opaque and cooked. Lift the fish onto a large serving platter.

4 Transfer the roasting tin of vegetables to the stove top and heat for a couple of minutes, until the juices bubble and reduce. Now add the cream and cook for 1 minute, then stir in the chervil and season to taste. Spoon the vegetables around the fish on the platter, pour over a little of the juice and hand around the rest separately in a jug.

SALT PORK WITH LENTILS

SERVES 6

1 kg (2 lb 4 oz) salt pork belly, cut into thick strips

1 small salt pork knuckle

1 large carrot, cut into chunks

200 g (7 oz) swede (rutabaga) or turnip, peeled and cut into chunks

100 g (4 oz) leek, white part only, thickly sliced

1 parsnip, cut into chunks

1 onion, studded with 4 cloves

1 garlic clove

1 bouquet garni

2 bay leaves

6 juniper berries, slightly crushed

350 g (12 oz) Puy lentils

2 tablespoons chopped flat-leaf (Italian) parsley

1 Depending on the saltiness of the pork you are using, you may need to soak it in cold water for several hours or blanch it before using. Ask your butcher whether to do this.

2 Put pork in a large saucepan with all the ingredients except the lentils and parsley. Stir thoroughly, then add just enough water to cover the ingredients. Bring to the boil, then reduce heat. Cover pan; leave to simmer gently for 1¼ hours.

3 Put the lentils in a sieve and rinse under cold running water. Add to the pan and stir, then cover and simmer for a further 45–50 minutes, or until the pork and lentils are tender.

4 Drain the pan into a colander, discarding the liquid and onion. Return the contents of the colander to the saucepan. Season to taste and stir in the parsley. Serve immediately.

BEEF CARBONNADE

SERVES 4

30 g (1 oz) butter

2–3 tablespoons oil

1 kg (2 lb 4 oz) lean beef rump or chuck
  steak, cubed

4 onions, chopped

1 garlic clove, crushed

1 teaspoon brown sugar

1 tablespoon plain (all-purpose) flour

500 ml (17 fl oz/2 cups) beer (bitter or
  stout)

2 bay leaves

4 thyme sprigs

CROUTONS

6–8 slices baguette

dijon mustard

1 Preheat the oven to 150°C (300°F/Gas 2). Melt the butter in a large sauté pan with a tablespoon of oil. Brown the meat in batches over high heat and then lift out onto a plate.

2 Add another tablespoon of oil to the pan and add the onion. Cook over moderate heat for 10 minutes, then add the garlic and sugar and cook for a further 5 minutes, adding another tablespoon of oil if necessary. Lift out the onion onto a second plate.

3 Reduce the heat to low and pour in any juices that have drained from the browned meat, then stir in the flour. Remove from the heat and stir in the beer, a little at a time (the beer will foam). Return to the heat and let the mixture gently simmer and thicken. Season with salt and pepper.

4 Layer the meat and onion in a casserole dish, tucking the bay leaves and sprigs of thyme between the layers and seasoning with salt and black pepper as you go. Pour the liquid over the meat, cover with a lid and cook in the oven for 2½–3 hours, or until the meat is tender.

5 To make the croutons, preheat the grill. Lightly toast the baguette on both sides, then spread one side with mustard. Arrange on top of the carbonnade, mustard side up, and place the whole casserole under the grill for a minute.

LAMB BRAISED WITH BEANS

SERVES 4

125 g (4½ oz) dried haricot beans

1 kg (2 lb 4 oz) shoulder of lamb boned, tied with string to keep its shape

30 g (1 oz) clarified butter or ghee (available from supermarkets)

2 carrots, diced

2 large onions, chopped

4 garlic cloves, unpeeled

1 bouquet garni

250 ml (9 fl oz/1 cup) dry red wine

250 ml (9 fl oz/1 cup) beef stock

1 Put beans in a large bowl and cover with plenty of water. Leave to soak for 8–12 hours, then drain. Bring a large saucepan of water to the boil, add the beans and return to the boil. Reduce the heat to moderate and cook the beans, partially covered, for 40 minutes. Drain well.

2 Rub the lamb all over with salt and pepper. Heat butter over high heat in a large flameproof casserole with a tight-fitting lid. Add the lamb and cook for 8–10 minutes, turning every few minutes until well browned. Remove the lamb.

3 Reheat the casserole over high heat and add the carrot, onion, garlic and bouquet garni. Reduce the heat and cook, stirring, for 8–10 minutes or until softened. Increase the heat to high and pour in the wine. Boil, stirring, for 30 seconds to deglaze, then return the lamb to the casserole. Add the stock.

4 Bring to the boil, then cover and reduce the heat to low. Braise the meat for 1½ hours, turning twice. If the lid is not tight fitting, cover casserole with foil and put the lid on top.

5 Add the cooked beans to the lamb and return to the boil over high heat. Reduce the heat to low, cover the casserole again and cook for a further 30 minutes.

6 Lift the lamb out of the casserole. cover and leave to rest for 10 minutes before carving. Discard the bouquet garni. Skim the excess fat from the surface of the sauce and, if the sauce is too thin, boil over high heat for 5 minutes or until thickened slightly. Taste for seasoning. Carve the lamb and arrange on a platter. Spoon the beans around the lamb and drizzle with the sauce. Serve the rest of the sauce separately.

BOEUF EN DAUBE

SERVES 6

1.5 kg (3 lb 5 oz) beef topside, blade or rump, cut into large pieces
2 tablespoons oil
3 strips pork fat
1 pig's trotter or 225 g (8 oz) piece bacon
750 ml (25 fl oz/3 cups) beef stock

MARINADE

2 cloves
1 onion, cut into quarters
500 ml (17 fl oz/2 cups) red wine
2 strips of orange zest
2 garlic cloves
½ celery stalk
2 bay leaves
a few parsley stalks

1   To make the marinade, push the cloves into a piece of onion and mix together in a large bowl with the remaining marinade ingredients. Season the beef with salt and pepper, add to the marinade and leave to marinate overnight.

2   Heat the oil in a saucepan. Lift the beef out of the marinade and pat dry, then brown in batches in the oil and remove to a plate. You might need to use a little of the marinade liquid to deglaze the pan between batches to prevent bits sticking to the bottom of the pan and burning.

3   Strain the marinade through a sieve into a bowl and tip the contents of the sieve into the pan to brown. Remove from the pan. Add the marinade liquid to the pan and boil, stirring, for 30 seconds to deglaze the pan.

4   Place the pork fat in a large casserole, then add the pig's trotter, beef and marinade ingredients. Pour in the marinade liquid and stock. Bring to the boil, then cover, reduce the heat and simmer gently for 2–2½ hours or until the meat is tender.

5   Lift the meat out of the casserole dish into a serving dish, cover and keep warm. Discard the garlic, onion, pork fat and pig's trotter. Pour the liquid through a fine sieve and skim off as much fat as possible, then return to the casserole. Bring to the boil and boil until reduced by half and syrupy. Pour the gravy over the meat to serve.

STEAK AU POIVRE

SERVES 4

4 x 200 g (7 oz) fillet steaks

2 tablespoons oil

6 tablespoons black peppercorns, crushed

40 g (1½ oz) butter

3 tablespoons Cognac

60 ml (2 fl oz/¼ cup) white wine

125 ml (4 fl oz/½ cup) thick (double/heavy) cream

1 Rub the steaks on both sides with the oil and press the crushed peppercorns into the meat. Melt the butter in a large frying pan and cook the steaks for 2–4 minutes on each side, depending on how you like your steak.

2 Add the Cognac and flambé by lighting the pan with your gas flame or a match (stand well back when you do this and keep a pan lid handy for emergencies). Put the steaks on a hot plate. Add the wine to the pan and boil, stirring, for 1 minute to deglaze the pan. Add the cream and stir for about 2 minutes. Season and pour over the steaks.

STEAK BÉARNAISE

SERVES 4

1 shallot, finely chopped

2 tablespoons white wine vinegar or tarragon vinegar

2 tablespoons white wine

3 tarragon sprigs

1 teaspoon dried tarragon

3 egg yolks

200 g (7 oz) clarified butter, melted

1 tablespoon chopped tarragon leaves

4 x 200 g (7 oz) fillet steaks

1 tablespoon oil

1 **Put the shallot,** vinegar, wine, tarragon sprigs and dried tarragon in a saucepan. Bring to the boil and cook until reduced to 1 tablespoon. Remove from heat and cool slightly.

2 **Whisk the egg yolks** with 1 tablespoon water, and add to the saucepan. Place the pan over very low heat or over a simmering bain-marie and continue to whisk until the sauce is thick. Do not boil or the eggs will scramble.

3 **Remove the sauce from the heat,** continue to whisk and slowly add the butter in a thin steady stream. Pass through a fine strainer, then stir in the chopped tarragon. Season with salt and pepper and keep warm while cooking the steaks.

4 **Rub the steaks with the oil,** season them with salt and pepper and cook for 2–4 minutes on each side, depending on how you like your steak. Serve with the sauce.

BOEUF EN CROUTE

SERVES 6

1 x 1 kg (2 lb 4 oz) thick beef fillet

30 g (1 oz) dripping or butter

1 quantity puff pastry (page 152)

1 egg, lightly beaten

PÂTÉ

180 g (7 oz) butter

3 shallots, chopped

1 garlic clove, chopped

360 g (12 oz) chicken livers

1 tablespoon brandy or Cognac

1 Preheat the oven to 220°C (425°F/Gas 7). To make the pâté, melt half the butter in a frying pan and add the shallots and garlic. Cook until softened but not browned.

2 Remove any discoloured spots from the chicken livers, wash and pat dry. Add the chicken livers to the frying pan and sauté for 4–5 minutes, or until cooked but still a little pink in the middle. Let the livers cool completely and then process in a food processor with the rest of the butter and the brandy. Alternatively, push the chopped livers through a sieve and mix with the butter and brandy. Season.

3 Tie the beef four or five times along its length to keep it in shape. Heat the dripping in a roasting tin and brown beef on all sides, then put in the oven and roast for 20 minutes. Allow to cool and remove the string.

4 Reduce oven temperature to 200°C (400°F/Gas 6). Roll the pastry into a rectangle just big enough to cover the beef fillet completely. Trim the edges and keep them for decoration. Spread the pâté over the pastry, leaving a border around the edge. Brush the border with beaten egg.

5 Lay the fillet on the pastry and wrap it up tightly like a parcel, pressing the seams together firmly and tucking the ends under. Put the parcel, seam side down, on a baking tray and brush all over with beaten egg. Cut pieces from the trimmings to decorate the pastry and brush with beaten egg. Bake for 25–30 minutes for rare and 35–40 minutes for medium. Allow the beef to rest for 5 minutes before carving.

ENTRECÔTE À LA BORDELAISE

SERVES 4

4 x 200 g (7 oz) entrecôte or sirloin
steaks

1½ tablespoons oil

SAUCE

50 g (2 oz), unsalted butter, chilled and
diced

3 French shallots, finely chopped

500 ml (17 fl oz/2 cups) red wine
(preferably Bordeaux)

250 ml (9 fl oz/1 cup) beef stock

80 g (3 oz) bone marrow

1 tablespoon chopped flat-leaf (Italian)
parsley

1 **To make the sauce,** melt 20 g (¾ oz) of the butter in a saucepan, add the shallot and cook, stirring, for 7 minutes or until very soft; do not allow shallot to brown. Pour in the wine and simmer until reduced by two-thirds. Add the stock and bone marrow and simmer until reduced by half, breaking up the marrow as it cooks.

2 **Whisk in remaining butter.** Season to taste with salt and pepper. Add the parsley.

3 **Trim and season the steaks** and rub with some of the oil. Heat the remaining oil in a frying pan, and cook the steaks for 2–4 minutes on each side, or until cooked to your liking. Pour the sauce over the top to serve.

PORK WITH SAGE AND CAPERS

SERVES 4–6

25 g (1 oz) unsalted butter

3 tablespoons extra virgin olive oil

1 onion, finely chopped

100 g (4 oz/1¼ cups) fresh white breadcrumbs

2 teaspoons chopped sage

1 tablespoon flat-leaf (Italian) parsley, chopped

2 teaspoons lemon zest, grated

2½ tablespoons capers, rinsed and drained

1 egg

2 large (about 500 g/1 lb 2 oz) pork fillets

8 large thin slices bacon or prosciutto

2 teaspoons plain (all-purpose) flour

100 ml (4 fl oz) dry vermouth

315 ml (10 fl oz/1¼ cups) chicken or vegetable stock

8 whole sage leaves, extra, to garnish

1 **Preheat oven to 170°C** (325°F/Gas 3). Heat the butter and 1 tablespoon of the oil in a frying pan. Add the onion and cook for 5 minutes, or until lightly golden.

2 **Put breadcrumbs,** sage, parsley, lemon zest, the cooked onion and ½ tablespoon capers in a bowl. Add the egg, season well and mix to combine.

3 **With a sharp knife,** split each pork fillet in half lengthways; take care not to cut all the way through, and open out. Spread the stuffing down the length of one; cover with the other fillet.

4 **Stretch the bacon or prosciutto** with the back of a knife and wrap each piece, overlapping slices slightly, around the pork to form a neat parcel. Tie with string at regular intervals.

5 **Place the pork** in a flameproof baking dish and drizzle with 1 tablespoon of oil. Bake for 1 hour. To test if the meat is cooked, insert a skewer in the thickest part; the juices should run clear. Remove the meat from the dish, cover with foil and leave to rest. Place the baking dish on the stovetop, add the flour and stir in well. Add the vermouth and allow to bubble for 1 minute. Add the stock and stir while cooking to remove all the lumps. Simmer for 5 minutes. Add the remaining capers to the sauce.

6 **In a small saucepan,** heat the remaining oil and when very hot, fry the sage leaves until crisp. Drain on paper towels.

7 **Slice the pork** into 2.5 cm (1 inch) slices. Spoon a little sauce over the pork. Serve each portion with fried sage leaves.

BLANQUETTE DE VEAU

SERVES 6

800 g (1 lb 12 oz) boneless veal shoulder, cut into 3 cm (1¼ in) cubes

1 litre (35 fl oz/4 cups) brown stock

4 cloves

½ large onion

1 small carrot, roughly chopped

1 leek, white part only, roughly chopped

1 celery stalk, roughly chopped

1 bay leaf

30 g (1 oz) butter

30 g (1 oz) plain (all-purpose) flour

1 tablespoon lemon juice

1 egg yolk

50 ml (2 fl oz/¼ cup) thick (double/heavy) cream

ONION GARNISH

250 g (9 oz) pickling or pearl onions

10 g (½ oz) butter

1 teaspoon caster (superfine) sugar

MUSHROOM GARNISH

10 g (½ oz) butter

2 teaspoons (½ oz) lemon juice

150 g (6 oz) button mushrooms, trimmed

1 Put veal in a large saucepan, cover with cold water and bring to the boil. Drain, rinse well and drain again. Return to the pan and add the stock. Press the cloves into the onion and add to the pan with the remaining vegetables and bay leaf.

2 Bring to the boil, reduce the heat, cover and simmer for 40–60 minutes, or until the veal is tender. Skim the surface occasionally. Strain, reserving the cooking liquid and throwing away the vegetables. Keep the veal warm.

3 To make the onion garnish, put the onions in a small pan with enough water to half cover them. Add the butter and sugar. Place a crumpled piece of greaseproof paper directly over the onions. Bring to a simmer. Cook over a low heat for about 20 minutes, or until the water has evaporated and the onions are tender.

4 To make the mushroom garnish, half-fill a small pan with water and bring to the boil. Add butter, lemon juice and mushrooms and simmer for 3 minutes, or until mushrooms are tender. Drain the mushrooms, discarding the liquid.

5 Heat the butter in a large saucepan. Stir in the flour to make a roux and cook, stirring, for 3 minutes without allowing the roux to brown. Remove from the heat and gradually add the cooking liquid from the veal, stirring after each addition until smooth. Return to the heat and whisk until the sauce comes to the boil, then reduce the heat to low and simmer for 8 minutes, or until the sauce coats the back of the spoon.

6 Add the lemon juice and season well. Quickly stir in the egg yolk and cream, then add the veal and the onion and mushroom garnishes. Reheat gently, without boiling, to serve.

ROAST VEAL STUFFED WITH HAM AND SPINACH

SERVES 4

250 g (9 oz) spinach leaves

2 garlic cloves, crushed

2 tablespoons finely chopped parsley

2 teaspoons dijon mustard

100 g (4 oz) ham on the bone, diced

finely grated zest of 1 lemon

1 x 600 g (1 lb 5 oz) piece boneless veal loin or fillet, beaten with a meat mallet to measure 30 x 15 cm (12 x 6 inches); ask your butcher to do this

4 bacon slices

2 tablespoons olive oil

50 g (2 oz) butter

16 baby carrots

8 small potatoes, unpeeled

8 shallots

200 ml (7 fl oz) dry Madeira (or other fortified wine such as sherry)

1 Preheat the oven to 170°C (325°F/Gas 3). Wash spinach and put in a large saucepan with just the water clinging to the leaves. Cover the pan and steam the spinach for 2 minutes or until just wilted. Drain, cool and squeeze dry. Chop and mix with garlic, parsley, mustard, ham and lemon zest. Season well.

2 Spread the spinach filling over the centre of the piece of veal. Starting from one of the shorter sides, roll up like a swiss roll. Wrap the slices of bacon over the meat and season well. Tie with string several times along the roll to secure the bacon and make sure the roll doesn't unravel.

3 Heat olive oil and half the butter in a large frying pan. Add carrots, potatoes and shallots. Briefly brown vegetables; tip into a roasting tin. Brown veal parcel on all sides, then place on top of vegetables. Add 4 tablespoons of Madeira to the pan and boil, stirring, for 30 seconds to deglaze pan. Pour over the veal.

4 Roast the meat for 30 minutes, then cover the top with foil to prevent overbrowning. Roast for another 45–60 minutes or until the juices run clear when you pierce the thickest part of the meat with a skewer. Wrap the meat in foil and leave to rest. Test the vegetables and return to the oven for a while if they're not yet tender. Remove them from the tin.

5 Place the roasting tin over moderate heat and add the rest of the Madeira. Allow it to bubble, then add the rest of the butter and season the sauce to taste. Slice the veal thickly and arrange the slices of meat on top of the vegetables. Pour over some of the Madeira sauce. Serve the rest separately in a jug.

PORK NOISETTES WITH PRUNES

SERVES 4

8 pork noisettes or 2 x 400 g (14 oz)
    pork fillets

16 prunes, pitted

1 tablespoon oil

45 g (1½ oz) butter

1 onion, finely chopped

155 ml (5 fl oz) white wine

280 ml (9½ fl oz) chicken or brown
    stock

1 bay leaf

2 thyme sprigs

250 ml (9 fl oz/1 cup) thick (double/
    heavy) cream

1 **Trim any excess fat from pork,** making sure you get rid of any membrane that will cause the pork to shrink. If using pork fillet, cut each one into four diagonal slices. Put the prunes in a small saucepan, cover with cold water and bring to the boil. Reduce heat and simmer the prunes for 5 minutes. Drain well.

2 **Heat the oil** in a large heavy-based frying pan and add half the butter. When the butter starts foaming, add the pork, in batches, if necessary, and sauté on both sides until cooked. Transfer the pork to a warm plate, cover and keep warm.

3 **Pour off excess fat** from the pan. Melt the remaining butter, add the onion and cook over low heat until softened but not browned. Add the wine, bring to the boil and simmer for 2 minutes. Add the stock, bay leaf and thyme and bring to the boil. Reduce the heat and simmer for 10 minutes or until reduced by half.

4 **Strain the stock** into a bowl and rinse the frying pan. Return the stock to the pan, add the cream and prunes and simmer for 8 minutes, or until sauce thickens slightly. Tip the pork back into the pan and simmer until heated through.

VEAL PAUPIETTES

SERVES 4

4 x 150 g (5½ oz) veal escalopes

STUFFING

30 g (1 oz) butter

2 French shallots, finely chopped

1 garlic clove, crushed

200 g (7 oz) minced (ground) pork

200 g (7 oz) minced (ground) veal

1 egg

2 tablespoons dry white wine

3 tablespoons fresh white breadcrumbs

2 tablespoons finely chopped flat-leaf (Italian) parsley

SAUCE

30 g (1 oz) clarified butter

1 onion, diced

1 carrot, diced

1 stalk celery, diced

100 ml (4 fl oz) white wine

2 teaspoons tomato paste (concentrated purée)

1 bay leaf

350 ml (12 fl oz) beef stock

1 **To make the stuffing,** melt the butter in a saucepan and cook the shallots over low heat until softened but not browned. Add garlic and cook for a further 2 minutes, then set aside to cool. Mix with the other stuffing ingredients and season with salt and pepper.

2 **Pound the veal escalopes flat** and spread evenly with the stuffing, leaving a border around the edge. Roll up the paupiettes, then tie with kitchen string at regular intervals.

3 **To make the sauce,** melt half the clarified butter in a frying pan. Add onion, carrot and celery and cook over low heat until softened. Increase heat to brown the vegetables. Remove from the pan.

4 **Heat remaining clarified butter** in the frying pan and brown the paupiettes, turning once. Remove from the pan, pour in the white wine and boil, stirring, for 30 seconds. Add the tomato paste and bay leaf. Pour in the stock and bring to a simmer before adding the vegetables and paupiettes.

5 **Cover the pan** and cook for 12–15 minutes, or until a skewer inserted into the centre of a paupiette comes out too hot to touch. Remove paupiettes from the pan; keep warm.

6 **Strain the sauce.** Return the sauce to the pan and boil until reduced by half and syrupy. Slice each paupiette into five pieces and serve with a little sauce poured over the top.

ROAST LEG OF LAMB WITH SPRING VEGETABLES

SERVES 6

1 x 2 kg (4 lb 8 oz) leg of lamb
3 rosemary sprigs
6 garlic cloves, unpeeled
500 g (1 lb 2 oz) small potatoes, halved
250 g (10 oz) baby carrots
6 small leeks
250 g (10 oz) small zucchini (courgettes)
1½ tablespoons plain (all-purpose) flour
150 ml (5 fl oz) red wine
150 ml (5 fl oz) brown stock

1   Preheat the oven to 200°C (400°F/Gas 6). Rub the lamb all over with salt and pepper. Put lamb in a roasting tin, lay the rosemary sprigs on top and scatter the garlic around the lamb. Roast for 20 minutes, then turn the lamb over.

2   Add the potatoes to the roasting tin and toss in the lamb fat, then return to the oven for a further 15 minutes. Turn the lamb again and cook for another 15 minutes.

3   Add the baby carrots and leeks to the tin, toss with the potatoes in the lamb fat and turn the lamb again. Roast for 15 minutes, then add the courgettes. Toss all the vegetables in the lamb fat and turn the leg of lamb again.

4   Roast for another 15 minutes, then lift the lamb out of the roasting tin to rest. The lamb will be rare — if you prefer, cook it for another 5–10 minutes. Remove the vegetables and garlic from the tin and keep warm.

5   To make the gravy, spoon the fat from the surface of the meat juices. Place the roasting tin over moderate heat on the stovetop and stir in the flour to make a roux. Cook, stirring, for 2 minutes, then gradually stir in the wine and stock. Boil the gravy for 2 minutes, then strain into a serving jug.

6   Carve the lamb and serve with the spring vegetables and garlic. Serve the gravy separately.

NAVARIN À LA PRINTANIÈRE

SERVES 6

1 kg (2 lb 4 oz) lean lamb shoulder

30 g (1 oz) butter

1 onion, chopped

1 garlic clove, crushed

1 tablespoon plain (all-purpose) flour

500 ml (17 fl oz/2 cups) brown stock

bouquet garni

18 baby carrots

8 large-bulb spring onions (scallions)

200 g (7 oz) baby turnips

175 g (6 oz) small potatoes

150 g (6 oz) peas, fresh or frozen

1 **Trim lamb of any fat and sinew** and then cut it into bite-sized pieces. Heat the butter over high heat in a large casserole. Brown the lamb in two or three batches, then remove from the casserole.

2 **Add the onion** to the casserole. Cook, stirring occasionally, over moderate heat for 3 minutes or until softened but not browned. Add garlic; cook a further minute, or until aromatic.

3 **Return the meat** and any juices to the casserole and sprinkle with the flour. Stir over high heat until meat is well coated and the liquid is bubbling, then gradually stir in the stock. Add the bouquet garni and bring to the boil. Reduce heat to low, cover the casserole and cook for 1¼ hours.

4 **Trim carrots,** leaving a little bit of green stalk. Do the same with the spring onions and baby turnips. Cut the potatoes in half if they are large.

5 **Add the vegetables** to the casserole dish, bring to the boil and simmer, covered, for 15 minutes or until the vegetables are tender. (If you are using frozen peas, add them right at the end so they just heat through.) Season with plenty of salt and pepper before serving.

LAMB STUFFED WITH COUSCOUS AND ALMONDS

SERVES 6

80 ml (3 fl oz/⅓ cup) olive oil

1 small red capsicum (pepper)

1 small yellow capsicum (pepper)

35 g (1 oz) whole blanched almonds

1 small onion, chopped

4 garlic cloves

100 g (4 oz) eggplant (aubergine), diced

400 g (14 oz) tin chopped tomatoes

pinch of sugar

1 tablespoon thyme leaves

2 teaspoons capers, rinsed and
   squeezed dry

8 black olives, pitted and finely chopped

50 g (2 oz) couscous

1 x 1.5 kg (3 lb 5 oz) tunnel-boned leg
   of lamb

½ small onion

GRAVY

1 tablespoon plain (all-purpose) flour

1 teaspoon tomato purée

275 ml (9½ fl oz) brown stock

100 ml (4 fl oz) red wine

1   Preheat oven to 200°C (400°F/Gas 6). Rub 1 tablespoon of oil over the capsicums and roast for 40–45 minutes, or until blackened. Cool, then peel the capsicums and cut into long thin strips.

2   Lightly toast the almonds in a dry frying pan, then chop. Heat 1 tablespoon of oil in the pan and cook the onion until softened. Crush 2 garlic cloves, add to the onion and cook for 5 minutes. Add 2 tablespoons of oil and the aubergine and cook for 10 minutes. Add the tomato and sugar and simmer until fairly dry. Remove from the heat and mix in the thyme, capers and olives. Cool.

3   Pour 100 ml boiling water onto the couscous. Leave for 5 minutes, then fluff the grains with a fork. Add the couscous, capsicums and almonds to the aubergine mixture; season well.

4   Increase oven to 230°C (450°F/Gas 8). Push as much stuffing as possibe into the cavity of the lamb. (Put any leftover stuffing in an ovenproof dish.) Fold the meat over the stuffing at each end and secure with skewers. Put the remaining cloves of garlic and the half onion in a roasting tin. Place the lamb on top. Roast for 30 minutes, then reduce the oven to 180°C (350°F/Gas 4) and cook for 1½ hours (cover with foil if overbrowning). Bake any extra stuffing for the last 20 minutes.

5   To make the gravy, remove the meat from the tin, cover and leave to rest. Strain off all but 2 tablespoons of fat from the tin, then place over moderate heat. Stir in flour and tomato purée and gradually add the stock, stirring. Add wine slowly, stirring until gravy reaches the consistency you like. Season well. Slice the meat and serve with gravy and extra stuffing.

SERVES 6

400 g (14 oz) dried haricot beans

bouquet garni

½ large onion, cut into quarters

2 garlic cloves, crushed

225 g (8 oz) salt pork or unsmoked bacon, cut into cubes

15 g (½ oz) clarified butter or ghee (available from supermarkets)

400 g (14 oz) lamb shoulder

350 g (12 oz) boiling sausages (saucisses à cuire), from specialty butchers

1 celery stalk, sliced

4 pieces duck confit or 4 pieces roasted duck

6 large tomatoes

180 g (7 oz) Toulouse sausage (from specialty butchers and delicatessens)

4 slices baguette, made into crumbs

1   Put the beans in a bowl and cover them with cold water. Soak overnight, then drain and rinse.

2   Put the beans in a large saucepan with the bouquet garni, onion, garlic and salt pork. Add 2–3 litres of cold water, bring to the boil and then simmer for 1 hour.

3   Heat the clarified butter in a frying pan. Cut the lamb into eight pieces and brown in the butter. Add lamb, boiling sausage, celery and duck confit to the top of the beans and push into the liquid. Score a cross in the top of each tomato, plunge into boiling water for 20 seconds, then peel skin away from the cross. Chop the tomatoes finely, discarding the cores, and add to the top of the cassoulet. Push into the liquid and cook for a further hour.

4   Brown the Toulouse sausage in the frying pan and add to the top of the cassoulet. Push into the liquid and cook for 30 minutes more. Preheat the oven to 160°C (315°f/gas 2–3).

5   Discard the bouquet garni. Strain the liquid into a saucepan and boil over moderate heat until reduced by two-thirds. Remove all the meat from the saucepan and slice the sausages and pull the duck meat from the bones. Layer the meat and beans, alternately, in a deep casserole. Pour in the liquid, to come no higher than the top of the beans.

6   Sprinkle the cassoulet with the breadcrumbs and bake for 40 minutes. Every 10 minutes, break the breadcrumb crust with the back of a spoon to let a little liquid come through. If the beans look a bit dry, add a little stock or water to the edge of the dish. Serve straight from the casserole.

GASCONNADE

SERVES 6

1 large leg of lamb, about 2.5 kg (5 lb), partially boned

1 carrot, coarsely chopped

1 stalk celery, coarsely chopped

1 large onion, coarsely chopped

1 bay leaf

1 bouquet garni

2 garlic cloves, crushed

6 anchovy fillets, mashed

½ tablespoon parsley, finely chopped

½ tablespoon thyme, finely chopped

½ tablespoon rosemary, finely chopped

3 tablespoons olive oil

25 garlic cloves, unpeeled

1 **Preheat oven** to 220°C (425°F/Gas 7). Place the removed lamb bone in a stockpot with the carrot, celery, onion, bay leaf and bouquet garni, and add just enough cold water to cover. Bring to the boil and simmer, uncovered, for 1 hour. Strain and if necessary, simmer until reduced to 500 ml (17 fl oz/2 cups).

2 **Meanwhile, combine the crushed garlic,** anchovies, chopped herbs and olive oil in a small bowl with some freshly ground black pepper. Rub the cavity of the lamb with most of the herb mixture. Roll the meat up and tie securely with kitchen string. Rub the lamb with the remaining herb mixture and place in a baking dish. Bake for 15 minutes, then reduce the temperature to moderate 180°C (350°F/Gas 4). Continue baking for about 45 minutes (for medium-rare), basting with the pan juices occasionally, until cooked to your liking.

3 **Bring a saucepan of water** to the boil and add the garlic cloves. Boil for 5 minutes. Drain and rinse under cold water. Peel the garlic and purée the pulp. Put it in the saucepan with the 2 cups (500 ml/16 fl oz) of stock. Bring to the boil, then simmer for 10 minutes. Transfer the lamb to a carving tray and keep warm. Spoon off fat from the pan juices. Add the garlic stock and place the dish over high heat. Bring to the boil and cook until reduced by half. Adjust the seasoning. Serve the lamb sliced, accompanied by the sauce.

BOEUF BOURGUIGNON

SERVES 6

1.5 kg (3 lb 5 oz) beef blade or chuck steak

750 ml (26 fl oz/3 cups) red wine

3 garlic cloves, crushed

bouquet garni

70 g (2 oz) butter

1 onion, chopped

1 carrot, chopped

2 tablespoons plain (all-purpose) flour

200 g (7 oz) bacon, cut into short strips

300 g (11 oz) shallots, peeled but left whole

200 g (7 oz) small button mushrooms

1   Cut the meat into 4 cm (1½ inch) cubes and trim away any excess fat. Put the meat, wine, garlic and bouquet garni in a large bowl, cover with plastic wrap and leave in the fridge for at least 3 hours and preferably overnight.

2   Preheat the oven to 160°C (315°F/Gas 2–3). Drain meat, reserving the marinade and bouquet garni. Dry the meat on paper towels. Heat 30 g (1 oz) of the butter in a large casserole dish. Add the onion, carrot and bouquet garni and cook over low heat, stirring occasionally, for 10 minutes. Remove from the heat.

3   Heat half the remaining butter in a large frying pan over high heat and fry the meat in batches for about 5 minutes or until well browned. Add to the casserole dish.

4   Pour the reserved marinade into the frying pan and boil, stirring, for 30 seconds to deglaze pan. Remove from the heat.

Return the casserole to high heat and sprinkle the meat and vegetables with the flour. Cook, stirring constantly, until the meat is well coated with the flour. Pour in the marinade and stir well. Bring to the boil, stirring constantly, then cover and cook in the oven for 2 hours.

5   Heat the remaining butter in the clean frying pan and cook the bacon and shallots, stirring, for 8–10 minutes or until shallots are softened but not browned. Add mushrooms and cook, stirring occasionally, for 2–3 minutes or until they are browned. Drain on paper towels. Add the shallots, bacon and mushrooms to the casserole.

6   Cover casserole and return to the oven for 30 minutes, or until the meat is soft and tender. Discard the bouquet garni. Season and skim any fat from the surface before serving.

POULE AU POT

SERVES 4

1 x 1.6 kg (3 lb 8 oz) chicken
1 carrot, roughly chopped
½ onion, halved
1 celery stalk, roughly chopped
1 garlic clove
4 parsley sprigs
2 bay leaves
8 black peppercorns
8 juniper berries
2 bacon bones
1 teaspoon salt
12 baby carrots
8 baby leeks
8 baby turnips
12 small new potatoes

1 Season the chicken and wrap it in muslin (cheesecloth), securing it with string. Place in a large saucepan. Tie the carrot, onion, celery, garlic, parsley, bay leaves, peppercorns and juniper berries in another piece of muslin and add to the pan. Add the bacon bones and salt, cover with cold water and bring to simmering point. Cook over very low heat for 40 minutes.

2 Trim the baby vegetables, add to the saucepan and cook for 10 more minutes. Lift out the chicken and drain on a wire rack over a tray. Cook the vegetables for a further 10 minutes. Remove the skin from the chicken and carve, then serve with the cooked vegetables. Strain the cooking liquid, discarding the bacon bones, and serve as a broth to start the meal or freeze for soup stock.

BIFTECK HACHÉ

SERVES 4

35 g (1 oz) butter

1 garlic clove, crushed

1 small onion, finely chopped

500 g (1 lb 2 oz) lean beef steak, minced

1 tablespoon finely chopped parsley

large pinch of grated nutmeg

1 large egg, lightly beaten

1 tablespoon oil

1 Melt 10 g of the butter in a saucepan and gently cook the garlic and onion for 10–15 minutes, or until the onion is softened but not browned. Cool.

2 Put the minced steak in a large bowl and add the onion mixture, parsley, nutmeg, beaten egg and plenty of ground black pepper. Combine well, then divide the mixture into four and roll into four balls. Put the balls on a large plate and gently pat each one down into a burger shape. Cover and chill in the fridge for at least 1 hour.

3 Melt the remaining butter and the oil in a frying pan, slide in the burgers and season with salt. Cook for 10–12 minutes over moderate heat, turning them halfway through. Burgers should be crusty on the outside and slightly pink on the inside. Serve with salad and frites.

PORK CHOPS WITH CALVADOS

SERVES 4

60 g (2 oz) butter

2 dessert apples, cored, each cut into 8 wedges

½ teaspoon sugar

1½ tablespoons oil

4 x 200 g (7 oz) pork chops, trimmed

45 ml (1½ oz) Calvados

2 shallots, finely chopped

250 ml (9 fl oz/1 cup) dry cider

125 ml (4 fl oz/½ cup) chicken stock

150 ml (6 fl oz/⅔ cup) thick (double/heavy) cream

1 Melt half the butter in a frying pan, add the apple and sprinkle with the sugar. Cook over low heat, turning occasionally, until tender and glazed.

2 Heat the oil in a frying pan and sauté the pork chops until cooked, turning once. Pour the excess fat from the pan, add the calvados and flambé by lighting the pan with your gas flame or a match (stand well back when you do this and keep a pan lid handy for emergencies). Transfer the pork to a plate and keep warm.

3 Add remaining butter to the pan and cook the shallot until soft but not brown. Add the cider, stock and cream and bring to the boil. Reduce the heat and simmer for 15 minutes, or until reduced enough to coat the back of a spoon.

4 Season the sauce, add the pork and simmer for 3 minutes to heat through. Serve with the apple.

POT AU FEU

SERVES 4

1 tablespoon oil

1 celery stalk, roughly chopped

2 carrots, roughly chopped

½ onion, roughly chopped

800 g (1 lb 12 oz) beef shank with marrowbone

1 x 600 g (1 lb 5 oz) piece beef chuck

2 bay leaves

4 thyme sprigs

a few parsley stalks

10 peppercorns

800 g (1 lb 12 oz) beef short ribs

VEGETABLE GARNISH

1 large celery stalk

350 g (12 oz) small potatoes

300 g (11 oz) baby carrots, green tops trimmed

200 g (7 oz) baby turnips

350 g (12 oz) baby leeks

dijon mustard and coarse sea salt, to serve

---

1 Heat the oil in a heavy-based frying pan and cook the chopped celery, carrot and onion over moderately high heat for 10 minutes, or until browned.

2 Remove the meat from the beef shank and reserve the marrowbone. Tie the beef chuck with string, like a parcel.

3 In a large saucepan, pour 3 litres (105 fl oz/12 cups) water, and bring to the boil. Add the browned vegetables, herbs, peppercorns, beef shank meat, ribs and beef chuck to the pan. Return to the boil; skim off any fat on the surface. Reduce heat, and simmer for 2–2½ hours, or until meat is very tender.

4 Gently transfer the meat to a clean saucepan and strain the cooking liquid over it. Discard vegetables. Season the meat with salt and pepper, add the marrowbone and simmer over moderate heat for about 10 minutes. Remove marrowbone, gently push marrow out of the bone and slice into six pieces.

5 To make the vegetable garnish, cut the celery into 5 cm (2 inch) lengths, then cut each piece in half lengthways. Cook the potatoes in salted boiling water for 10 minutes, or until tender to the point of a knife, then drain. Add the celery, carrots, turnips and leeks to the meat and cook for 7 minutes. Add potatoes and cook for another 3 minutes to heat through.

6 Slice meats and serve with the marrow and vegetables. Serve the broth separately in bowls, accompanied by plenty of mustard and sea salt.

FISH COOKED IN PAPER

SERVES 4

4 skinless fish fillets, 200 g/7 oz each
(e.g. John dory, orange roughy,
snapper, bream)

1 leek, white part only, sliced into very
thin srips

4 spring onions (scallions), finely
chopped

30 g (1 oz) butter, softened

1 lemon, cut into 12 very thin slices

2–3 tablespoons lemon juice

1 **Preheat the oven** to moderate 180°C (350°F/ Gas 4). Place each fish fillet in the centre of a piece of baking paper large enough to enclose it. Season lightly.

2 **Scatter with the leek** and spring onion. Top each with a teaspoon of butter and 3 slices of lemon. Sprinkle with the extra lemon juice. Bring the paper together and fold it over several times. Fold the ends under to make parcels. Bake on a baking tray for 20 minutes (the steam will make the paper puff up). Check to see that the fish is cooked (it should be white and flake easily when tested with a fork). Serve each piece of fish in its parcel or lift it out and pour the juices over it.

OCTOPUS BRAISED IN TOMATO AND WINE

SERVES 6

500 g (1 lb 2 oz) ripe tomatoes

1 kg (2 lb 4 oz) baby octopus

60 ml (2 fl oz/¼ cup) olive oil

1 large brown onion, chopped

2 garlic cloves

350 ml (11 fl oz/1⅓ cups) dry white wine

¼ teaspoon saffron threads

2 sprigs fresh thyme

2 tablespoons roughly chopped flat-leaf (Italian) parsley

1 Score a cross in the base of each tomato. Place tomatoes in a bowl of boiling water for 20 seconds, then plunge them into cold water and peel skin away from the cross. Cut each tomato in half, scoop out the seeds with a teaspoon and chop the flesh.

2 To clean each octopus, use a small sharp knife and cut each head from the tentacles. Remove the eyes by cutting a round of flesh from the base of each head. To clean the heads, carefully slit them open and remove the gut. Rinse thoroughly. Cut the heads in half. Push out the beaks from the centre of the tentacles from the cut side. Cut tentacles into sets of four or two, depending on the size of the octopus.

3 Blanch all the octopus in boiling water for 2 minutes then drain and allow to cool slightly. Pat dry with paper towels.

4 Heat the olive oil in a heavy-based frying pan and cook the onion for 7–8 minutes over medium heat until lightly golden. Add octopus and garlic to the pan. Cook for another 2–3 minutes. Add the tomato, wine, saffron and thyme and just enough water to cover the octopus.

5 Simmer, covered, for 1 hour. Uncover and cook for another 15 minutes, or until the octopus is tender and the sauce has thickened a little. The cooking time will vary quite a bit depending on the size of the octopus. Season, to taste. Serve hot or at room temperature, sprinkled with parsley.

LAMB AND ARTICHOKE FRICASSEE

SERVES 8

6 fresh globe artichokes (see Note)

60 ml (2 fl oz/¼ cup) lemon juice

2 large, ripe tomatoes

80 ml (2¾ fl oz/⅓ cup) olive oil

2 kg (4 lb 8 oz) diced lamb

750 g (1 lb 8 oz) brown onions, thinly sliced

1 tablespoon plain (all-purpose) flour

2 garlic cloves, crushed

185 ml (16 fl oz/¾ cup) white wine

350 ml (11 fl oz/1⅓ cups) chicken stock

1 bouquet garni

chopped flat-leaf (Italian) parsley, to garnish

lemon wedges, for serving

1 **To prepare the globe artichokes,** bring a large saucepan of water to the boil and add the lemon juice. Trim the stems from the artichokes and remove the tough outer leaves. Cut off the hard tips of the remaining leaves using scissors. Blanch the artichokes for 5 minutes. Remove and turn upside-down to drain. When cool enough to handle, use a small spoon to remove the choke from the centre of each. Scrape the bases well to remove all the membrane. Cut the artichokes into quarters and set aside.

2 **Score a cross** in the base of each tomato and place in a bowl of boiling water for 20 seconds. Then plunge them into cold water and peel away from the cross. Cut each tomato in half, scoop out the seeds with a teaspoon and chop the flesh.

3 **Heat half the oil** in a deep heatproof casserole and fry batches of the lamb until golden. Add remaining oil and cook the onion for about 8 minutes, until soft and caramelized. Add the flour and cook for 1 minute. Add the garlic, tomato, wine and chicken stock. Return the lamb to the pan add the bouquet garni and simmer, covered, for 1 hour.

4 **Place artichokes** in the casserole and simmer, uncovered, for another 15 minutes. Remove meat and artichokes with a slotted spoon and place in a serving dish. Keep warm. Discard bouquet garni. Cook the sauce over high heat until it thickens. Pour the sauce over the lamb and garnish with parsley. Serve with lemon wedges.

Note: If fresh artichokes are not available, you can use 270 g (9 oz/1 cup) marinated artichokes. Drain them well and pat dry.

BEEF PROVENÇALE

SERVES 6

1.5 kg (3 lb 5 oz) chuck steak, cut into 3 cm (1¼ inch) cubes

2 tablespoons olive oil

1 small onion, sliced

375 ml (13 fl oz/1½ cups) red wine

2 tablespoons chopped flat-leaf (Italian) parsley

1 tablespoon chopped rosemary

1 tablespoon chopped thyme

2 bay leaves

250 g (9 oz) speck (from specialty butchers and delicatessens), rind removed, cut into 1 x 2 cm (½ x ¾ inch) pieces

400 g (14 oz) tinned crushed tomatoes

250 ml (9 fl oz/1 cup) beef stock

500 g (1 lb 2 oz) baby carrots

45 g (1¾ oz/⅓ cup) pitted niçoise olives or other small olive

1 Place the cubed beef, 1 tablespoon of the oil, the onion, 250 ml (9 fl oz/1 cup) of wine and half the herbs in a bowl. Cover with plastic wrap and marinate in refrigerator overnight. Drain the beef, reserving the marinade. Heat the remaining oil in a large heavy-based saucepan and brown the beef and onion in batches. Remove from the pan.

2 Add speck to the pan and cook for 3–5 minutes, or until crisp. Return the beef to the pan with the remaining wine and marinade and cook, scraping the residue from the base of the pan for 2 minutes, or until the wine has slightly reduced. Add the tomato and stock and bring to the boil. Reduce the heat and add the remaining herbs. Season well, cover and simmer for 1½ hours.

3 Add the carrots and olives to the saucepan and cook, uncovered, for another 30 minutes, or until the meat and the carrots are tender. Before serving, check the seasoning and adjust if necessary.

CHICKEN AND BACON GOUGÈRE

SERVES 6

60 g (2 oz) butter

1–2 garlic cloves, crushed

1 red onion, chopped

3 bacon slices, chopped

30 g (1 oz/¼ cup) plain (all-purpose) flour

375 ml (13 fl oz/1½ cups) milk

125 ml (4 fl oz/½ cup) pouring cream

2 teaspoons wholegrain mustard

250 g (9 oz) cooked chicken, chopped

30 g (1 oz) chopped parsley

CHOUX PASTRY

60 g (2 oz/½ cup) plain (all-purpose) flour

60 g (2 oz) chilled butter, cubed

2 eggs, lightly beaten

35 g (1 oz/⅓ cup) freshly grated parmesan cheese

1 Melt the butter in a frying pan, add the garlic, onion and bacon and cook for 5–7 minutes, stirring occasionally, or until cooked but not brown. Stir in the flour and cook for 1 minute. Gradually add the milk and stir until thickened. Simmer for 2 minutes, then add the cream and mustard. Remove from the heat and fold in the chicken and parsley. Season with pepper.

2 To make choux pastry, sift flour onto a piece of baking paper. Put the butter in a large saucepan with 125 ml (4 fl oz/½ cup) water and stir over medium heat until the mixture comes to the boil. Remove from the heat, add the flour in one go and quickly beat it into the water with a wooden spoon. Return to the heat and continue beating until the mixture forms a ball and leaves the side of the pan. Transfer to a large clean bowl and cool slightly. Beat the mixture to release any more heat. Gradually add the beaten egg, about 3 teaspoons

at a time. Beat well after each addition until all the egg has been added and the mixture is thick and glossy — a wooden spoon should stand up in it. If it is too runny, the egg has been added too quickly. If so, beat for several minutes more, or until thickened. Add the parmesan.

3 Preheat oven to 210°C (415°F/Gas 6–7). Grease a deep 23 cm (9 inch) ovenproof dish, pour in the filling and spoon heaped tablespoons of choux around the outside. Bake for 10 minutes, then reduce the oven to 180°C (350°F/Gas 4). Bake for 20 minutes, or until the choux is puffed and golden. Sprinkle with a little more grated parmesan if desired.

POULET VALLÉE D'AUGE

SERVES 4

1 x 1.6 kg (3 lb 8 oz) chicken

2 dessert apples

1 tablespoon lemon juice

60 g (2 oz) butter

½ onion, finely chopped

½ celery stalk, finely chopped

10 g (½ oz) plain (all-purpose) flour

80 ml (3 fl oz/⅓ cup) Calvados or brandy

375 ml (13 fl oz/1½ cups) chicken stock

100 ml (4 fl oz) crème fraîche or sour cream

1 Joint chicken into eight pieces by removing both legs and cutting between the joint of the drumstick and the thigh. Cut down either side of the backbone and lift it out. Turn the chicken over and cut through the cartilage down the centre of the breastbone. Cut each breast in half, leaving the wing attached to the top half.

2 Peel and core the apples. Finely chop half of one apple and cut the rest into 12 wedges. Toss in the lemon juice.

3 Heat half the butter in a large frying pan, add chicken pieces, skin side down, and cook until golden. Turn over and cook for another 5 minutes. Lift chicken out of the pan and tip away the fat.

4 In the same pan, heat 20 g (1 oz) more butter, add the onion, celery and chopped apple and fry over moderate heat for 5 minutes without browning.

5 Remove from the heat. Sprinkle flour over the vegetables and stir in. Add the calvados and return to the heat. Gradually stir in the chicken stock. Bring to the boil, return the chicken to the pan, cover and simmer gently for 15 minutes, or until the chicken is tender and cooked through.

6 Heat the remaining butter in a small frying pan, add the apple wedges and fry over moderate heat until browned and tender. Remove from the pan and keep warm.

7 Remove chicken from pan and keep warm. Skim the excess fat from the cooking liquid. Add the crème fraîche, bring to the boil and boil for 4 minutes, or until the sauce is thick enough to lightly coat the back of a wooden spoon. Season and pour over the chicken. Serve with apple wedges.

SALADS
& SIDES

ROASTED FENNEL AND ORANGE SALAD

SERVES 4

8 small bulbs fennel

100 ml (4 fl oz) olive oil

2 oranges

1 tablespoon lemon juice

1 red onion, halved and thinly sliced

100 g (4 oz) kalamata olives

2 tablespoons mint, roughly chopped

1 tablespoon roughly chopped flat-leaf (Italian) parsley

1 Preheat the oven to 200°C (400°F/Gas 6). Trim fronds from the fennel and reserve. Remove stalks and cut a slice off the base of each fennel bulb about 5 mm (¼ inch) thick. Slice each bulb into six wedges, place in a baking dish and drizzle with 3 tablespoons olive oil. Season well. Bake 40–45 minutes, or until fennel is tender and slightly caramelized. Turn once or twice during cooking. Allow to cool.

2 Cut a thin slice off the top and bottom of each orange, with a small, sharp knife. Slice the skin and pith off the oranges, removing as much pith as possible. Slice down the side of a segment between the flesh and the membrane. Repeat with the other side and lift the segment out. Do this over a bowl to catch the juices. Repeat with all the segments. Squeeze any juice remaining in the membranes into the bowl.

3 Whisk the remaining oil into the orange juice and the lemon juice and season well. Combine the orange segments, onion and olives in a bowl, add half the dressing and half the mint. Mix well. Transfer to a serving dish. Top with the roasted fennel, drizzle with remaining dressing and scatter the parsley and remaining mint over the top. Chop the reserved fronds and sprinkle over the salad.

SALAD WITH CHÈVRE

SERVES 4

50 g (2 oz) walnuts, broken into pieces

1 teaspoon flaked sea salt

8 slices baguette

1 garlic clove, cut in half

125 g (5 oz) chèvre (see Note), cut into
  8 slices

50 g (2 oz) mesclun (mixed salad leaves
  and herbs)

1 small red onion, thinly sliced

DRESSING

2 tablespoons olive oil

1 tablespoon walnut oil

1½ tablespoons tarragon vinegar

1 garlic clove, crushed

1 Preheat the grill (broiler) to hot. Put walnuts in a bowl and cover with boiling water. Leave for 1 minute, then drain and shake dry. Toast under the grill for 3–4 minutes, or until golden. Sprinkle with sea salt, toss lightly and allow to cool.

2 Put the baguette slices under the grill and toast one side until lightly golden. Remove from the heat and rub the toasted side with cut garlic. Leave to cool and crisp for a few minutes, turn over and place a slice of chèvre on each. Grill for about 3 minutes, or until the cheese browns.

3 To make the dressing, combine the olive oil, walnut oil, vinegar and garlic and season well.

4 Toss the mesclun, onion and toasted walnuts together on a large platter. Arrange the chèvre croutons on top and drizzle with the dressing. Serve while the croutons are still warm.

Note: Chèvre is goat's cheese, which has a pleasant, tangy flavour and a soft, smooth texture. Chèvre teams beautifully with the rich crunch of toasted walnuts and the freshness of salad greens. This salad works best when plated individually rather than served from a large bowl.

SALADE WITH WALNUTS

SERVES 4

4 thin baguette slices (or other long bread stick)

1 garlic clove, cut in half

4 tablespoons olive oil

1 large butter lettuce

25 ml (1 fl oz) walnut oil

25 ml (1 fl oz) red wine vinegar

1 teaspoon dijon mustard

70 g (2 oz) walnuts, broken into pieces

150 g (6 oz) bacon slices, cut into small pieces

1 **Preheat the grill (broiler)** and rub the baguette with the cut garlic. Drizzle a little of the olive oil on each side of the bread and then grill until golden brown. Leave to cool.

2 **Tear the lettuce leaves** into pieces and arrange on a large platter. Mix together the remaining olive oil, walnut oil, vinegar and mustard and season to make a dressing.

3 **Put the walnuts in a bowl** and cover with boiling water. Leave for 1 minute, drain and shake dry.

4 **Cook the bacon** in a frying pan until crisp, remove from the pan with a slotted spoon and sprinkle over the lettuce. Add the walnuts to the pan and cook for a few minutes until browned, then add to the salad. Pour the dressing into the pan and heat through.

5 **Pour dressing over salad** and toss well to combine. Add the garlic croutons to serve.

SALADE NIÇOISE

SERVES 4

4 waxy potatoes

1 tablespoon olive oil

200 g (7 oz) small green beans, halved

300 g (11 oz) tinned tuna in oil, drained

200 g (7 oz) lettuce leaves

150 g (6 oz) cherry tomatoes, halved

20 black olives, pitted

2 tablespoons capers

3 hard-boiled eggs, cut into wedges

8 anchovy fillets

VINAIGRETTE

1 garlic clove, crushed

1 teaspoon dijon mustard

2 tablespoons white wine vinegar

1 teaspoon lemon juice

125 ml (4 fl oz/½ cup) olive oil

1 Cook the potatoes in boiling salted water for 15 minutes, or until just tender. Drain, cut into small cubes and place in a bowl. Drizzle with the olive oil and toss well. Cook the green beans in boiling salted water for 3 minutes, then drain. Refresh under cold water, then drain well.

2 For the vinaigrette, whisk together the garlic, mustard, vinegar and lemon juice. Add the oil in a thin steady stream, whisking until smooth.

3 Put the tuna in a bowl and separate into large chunks with a fork. Cover the base of a serving dish with the lettuce leaves. Scatter the potatoes, beans, tuna, tomatoes, olives and capers over the leaves, pour the vinaigrette over the top and decorate with the egg and anchovies.

SALADE LYONNAISE

SERVES 4 AS A STARTER

1 garlic clove, cut in half

oil, for shallow-frying

4 slices white bread, crusts removed, cut into 1 cm (½ inch) cubes

60 ml (2 fl oz/¼ cup) olive oil

2 spring onions (scallions), chopped

3 bacon slices, cut into short strips

80 ml (3 fl oz/⅓ cup) red wine vinegar

3 teaspoons wholegrain mustard

225 g (8 oz) frisée (endive),

lamb's lettuce (corn salad) and dandelion leaves

4 eggs

1 Rub the cut garlic over the base of a frying pan. Pour oil into the pan to a depth of 1 cm (½ inch). Fry the bread cubes for 1–2 minutes, or until golden. Drain on paper towels. Wipe out the pan.

2 Heat the olive oil in the frying pan and cook the spring onion and bacon for 2 minutes. Add the vinegar and mustard and boil for 2 minutes to reduce by a third. Pour over the salad leaves and toss to wilt a little. Arrange on serving plates.

3 To poach eggs, bring a pan of water to the boil. Crack each egg into a ramekin, reduce the heat and slide the eggs into the simmering water. Poach for 3 minutes, lift out with a slotted spoon and drain on paper towels. Place on the leaves and sprinkle with the croutons. Serve immediately.

FRISÉE AND GARLIC CROUTON SALAD

SERVES 4–6

1 tablespoon olive oil

250 g (9 oz) speck, rind removed, cut into 5 mm x 2 cm (¼ x ¾ inch) pieces

½ baguette (or other long bread stick), sliced

4 garlic cloves

1 baby frisée (curly endive)

100 g (4 oz) walnuts, toasted

VINAIGRETTE

1 French shallot, finely chopped

1 tablespoon dijon mustard

60 ml (2 fl oz/¼ cup) tarragon vinegar or other herb vinegar

170 ml (6 fl oz/⅔ cup) olive oil

1 To make the vinaigrette, whisk together the shallot, mustard and vinegar in a small bowl. Slowly add the oil, whisking constantly until thickened. Set aside.

2 Heat the oil in a large frying pan, add the speck, bread and garlic and cook over medium–high heat for 5–8 minutes, or until the bread and speck are both crisp. Remove the garlic from the pan.

3 Put the frisée, baguette, speck, walnuts and vinaigrette in a large bowl. Toss together well and serve.

MUSHROOMS WITH TARRAGON AND CRÈME FRAÎCHE

SERVES 4

80 ml (3 fl oz/⅓ cup) olive oil

2 tablespoons lemon juice

4 garlic cloves, crushed

12 large flat field mushrooms

2 tablespoons finely chopped flat-leaf
    (Italian) parsley

toasted bread, to serve

**TARRAGON AND LEMON CRÈME
FRAÎCHE**

60 g (2 oz/¼ cup) crème fraîche

2 teaspoons lemon juice

1 garlic clove, crushed

2 teaspoons chopped tarragon

1 **Preheat the oven to 200°C** (400°F/Gas 6). Put the olive oil, lemon juice and garlic in a large roasting tin.

2 **Wipe mushrooms** with paper towels and trim the stems. Add the mushrooms to the roasting tin and gently toss until coated. Arrange in a single layer and season well with sea salt and freshly cracked black pepper. Roast for 30 minutes, turning to cook evenly.

3 **In a small bowl,** combine all the ingredients for the tarragon and lemon crème fraîche.

4 **Sprinkle the hot mushrooms** and their cooking juices with the parsley. Serve with crème fraîche and toasted bread.

PEAS WITH ONIONS AND LETTUCE

SERVES 6

50 g (2 oz) butter

16 baby onions or French shallots

500 g (1 lb 2 oz) fresh shelled peas

250 g (9 oz) iceberg lettuce heart, finely shredded

2 sprigs flat-leaf (Italian) parsley

1 teaspoon caster (superfine) sugar

125 ml (4 fl oz/½ cup) chicken stock

1 tablespoon plain (all-purpose) flour

1 **In a large saucepan,** melt 30 g (1 oz) of butter. Add onions and cook, stirring, for 1 minute. Add peas, lettuce, parsley and sugar. Pour in the stock and stir well. Cover pan and cook over medium–low heat for 15 minutes, stirring occasionally, until onions are cooked through. Remove parsley.

2 **Mix the remaining butter** with the flour, then add small amounts to the vegetables, stirring until the juices thicken a little. Season well with salt and black pepper

BRAISED WITLOF

SERVES 4

8 heads witlof (chicory/Belgian endive)

20 g (1 oz) butter

1 teaspoon soft brown sugar

2 teaspoons tarragon vinegar

100 ml (4 fl oz) chicken stock

2 tablespoons thick (double/heavy)
 cream

1 **Trim the ends from the witlof.** Melt the butter in a deep frying pan and fry the witlof briefly on all sides. Add the sugar, vinegar and chicken stock and bring to the boil. Reduce the heat to a simmer and cover the pan.

2 **Simmer gently for 30 minutes,** or until tender, turning halfway through. Take the lid off the pan and simmer until nearly all the liquid has evaporated. Stir in the cream and serve.

LENTILS IN RED WINE

SERVES 4–6

2 tablespoons olive oil

1 stalk celery, finely diced

1 large carrot, finely diced

1 large onion, finely diced

2 garlic cloves, crushed

2 tablespoons tomato paste (concentrated purée)

280 g (10 oz/1½ cups) Puy lentils

250 ml (9 fl oz/1 cup) red wine

250 ml (9 fl oz/1 cup) beef stock

1 bay leaf, crushed

5 sprigs thyme

3 tablespoons chopped flat-leaf (Italian) parsley

1 **Heat olive oil** in a large, heavy-based saucepan. Add the celery, carrot and onion and cook over medium–low heat for 10 minutes. Add the garlic and cook for a further 2 minutes.

2 **Add tomato paste** and cook over low heat for 5 minutes. Stir in the lentils, then add the wine and cook over medium heat for 3–5 minutes, until slightly reduced. Add the stock and 375 ml (12 fl oz/1½ cups) water, bring to the boil, then reduce the heat and add the herbs. Season and simmer for about 45 minutes, until the liquid is absorbed and lentils are cooked. Stir in the parsley and serve.

PURÉE OF SPINACH

SERVES 4

1 kg (2 lb 4 oz) baby spinach leaves

50 g (2 oz) butter, cubed

4 tablespoons crème fraîche (see Note)

½ teaspoon nutmeg

1 **Wash the spinach** and put in a large saucepan with just the water clinging to the leaves. Cover and steam for 2 minutes, or until just wilted. Drain, cool and squeeze dry with your hands. Finely chop.

2 **Put the spinach** in a small saucepan and gently heat through. Increase the heat and, stirring constantly, gradually add butter. Add the crème fraîche and nutmeg and stir into the spinach to combine. Season well and serve immediately.

Note: Sour cream can be used in place of crème fraîche.

BOULANGÈRE POTATOES

SERVES 6

1 kg (2 lb 4 oz) all-purpose potatoes
1 large onion
2 tablespoons finely chopped parsley
500 ml (27 fl oz/2 cups) chicken stock
25 g (1 oz) butter
salt
black pepper

1 Preheat the oven to 180°C (350°F/Gas 4). Thinly slice the potatoes and the onion with a mandolin or sharp knife. Layer potato and onion alternately in a 20 x 10 cm (8 x 4 inch) deep dish, sprinkling parsley, salt and black pepper between each layer. Finish with a layer of potato.

2 Heat the chicken stock and pour over the top. Dot with butter. Bake, covered with foil, on the middle shelf of the oven for 30 minutes, then remove the foil and press down on the potatoes to keep them submerged in the stock. Bake a further 30 minutes, or until potatoes are tender and the top golden brown. Serve piping hot.

RATATOUILLE

SERVES 4

4 tomatoes

2 tablespoons olive oil

1 large onion, diced

1 red capsicum (pepper), diced

1 yellow capsicum (pepper), diced

1 eggplant (aubergine), diced

2 zucchini (courgettes), diced

1 teaspoon tomato paste (concentrated purée)

½ teaspoon sugar

1 bay leaf

3 sprigs thyme sprigs

2 sprigs basil sprigs

1 garlic clove, crushed

1 tablespoon chopped flat-leaf (Italian) parsley

1 Score a cross in the base of each tomato, then plunge them into boiling water for 20 seconds. Peel the skin away from the cross, and roughly chop the flesh.

2 Heat the oil in a frying pan. Add onion and cook over low heat for 5 minutes. Add capsicum and cook, stirring, for 4 minutes. Remove from the pan and set aside.

3 Fry eggplant until lightly browned all over, then remove from the pan. Fry zucchini until browned and then return the onion, capsicum and eggplant to the pan. Add tomato paste, stir well and cook for 2 minutes. Add the tomato, sugar, bay leaf, thyme and basil. Stir well, cover and cook for 15 minutes. Remove the bay leaf, thyme and basil.

4 Combine the garlic and parsley and add to the ratatouille at the last minute. Stir and serve.

TIAN OF POTATOES

SERVES 6–8

500 g (1 lb 2 oz) sweet potato

1.25 kg (2 lb 12 oz) all-purpose potatoes

4 large leeks

3 garlic cloves

¾ teaspoon nutmeg

3 bay leaves

300 ml (10½ fl oz) pouring cream

1 **Preheat the oven to 170°C** (325°F/Gas 3) and grease a 26 x 28 x 7 cm (10 x 11 x 3 inch) tian or shallow, ovenproof ceramic dish. Peel and thinly slice the sweet potato and potatoes. Slice leeks into thin rings. Thinly slice the garlic.

2 **Layer half the potatoes** over the base of the prepared dish. Scatter a few slices of garlic over them and add a bay leaf. Sprinkle lightly with salt and pepper, and ¼ teaspoon of the nutmeg. Scatter the leeks, some garlic slices and a bay leaf over the top. Sprinkle with salt and pepper and ¼ teaspoon of nutmeg. Layer the sweet potato, some garlic slices and a bay leaf and season as above with salt, pepper and nutmeg. Layer with the remaining potatoes, season and then pour the cream over the top.

3 **Bake for about 2½ hours,** covered with foil, or until the vegetables are very tender. After 2 hours, remove the foil to allow the top to become crisp and golden. Remove from the oven and rest for 5 minutes before serving.

FENNEL, TOMATO AND GARLIC GRATIN

SERVES 4

1 kg (2 lb 4 oz) fennel bulbs

4 tablespoons olive oil

1 large red onion, halved and thinly
sliced

2 garlic cloves, crushed

500 g (1 lb 2 oz) tomatoes

GRATIN TOPPING

60 g (2 oz) white bread, broken into
coarse crumbs

65 g (2¼ oz) parmesan cheese, grated

2 teaspoons grated lemon zest

1 garlic clove, crushed

1 **Preheat the oven to 200°C** (400°F/Gas 6). Grease an ovenproof dish with melted butter or oil. Cut the fennel in half lengthways, then slice thinly.

2 **Heat oil in a large frying pan** and cook the onion for 3–4 minutes until softened but not browned. Add the garlic and cook for 2 minutes. Add fennel and cook, stirring frequently, for 7 minutes, or until softened and lightly golden brown.

3 **Score a cross** in the base of each tomato, then plunge them into boiling water for 20 seconds. Peel the skin away from the cross. Chop the flesh roughly and add to the fennel. Cook, stirring frequently, for 5 minutes, or until the tomato is softened. Season well and pour into the dish.

4 **To make the gratin topping,** combine all the ingredients, sprinkle over the vegetables and bake for 15 minutes, or until golden brown and crisp. Serve immediately.

POTATOES ANNA

SERVES 4

850 g (1 lb 14 oz) boiling potatoes
125 g (5 oz) clarified butter or ghee, melted (available from supermarkets)

1 Preheat oven to 210°C (415°F/Gas 6–7). Grease a deep 20 cm (8 inch) round cake tin or ovenproof dish with the melted butter.

2 Peel potatoes and cut into very thin slices with a mandolin or sharp knife. Lay the potato slices on paper towels and pat dry. Starting from the centre of the dish, overlap one-fifth of the potato slices over the base. Drizzle one-fifth of the butter over the top. Season well.

3 Repeat the layers four more times, drizzling the last bit of butter over the top. Cut a circle of baking paper to fit over the top of the potato. Bake for about 1 hour, or until cooked and golden and a knife blade slides easily into the centre. Remove from the oven and leave for 5 minutes. Pour off any excess butter. Run a knife around the edge to loosen, then turn out onto a serving plate.

GRATIN DAUPHINOIS

SERVES 6

1 kg (2 lb 4 oz) roasting potatoes

2 garlic cloves, crushed

65 g (2 oz/½ cup) grated gruyère cheese

pinch of nutmeg

315 ml (11 fl oz/1¼ cups) thick (double/ heavy) cream

125 ml (4 fl oz/½ cup) milk

1 **Preheat the oven to 170°C** (325°F/Gas 3). Thinly slice the potatoes with a mandolin or sharp knife. Butter a 23 x 16 cm (9 x 6½ inch) ovenproof dish and layer the potatoes, sprinkling the garlic, grated cheese, nutmeg and seasoning between the layers and leaving a bit of cheese for the top. Pour the cream and milk over the top and sprinkle with the cheese.

2 **Bake for 50–60 minutes** or until potatoes are completely cooked and the liquid absorbed. If the top browns too much, cover loosely with foil. Leave for 10 minutes before serving.

VICHY CARROTS

SERVES 6

500 g (1 lb 2 oz) carrots

½ teaspoon salt

1½ teaspoons sugar

40 g (1½ oz) butter

1½ tablespoons chopped parsley

1   Slice the carrots quite thinly, then put in a deep frying pan. Cover with cold water and add the salt, sugar and butter. Simmer until the water has evaporated. Shake the pan to glaze the carrot. Add the parsley, toss together and serve.

VEGETABLE TIAN

SERVES 4

60 ml (2 fl oz/¼ cup) olive oil

500 g (1 lb 2 oz) zucchini (courgettes), thickly sliced on the diagonal

4 garlic cloves, crushed

pinch of nutmeg

650 g (1 lb 7 oz) tomatoes

2 red onions, chopped

60 ml (2 fl oz/¼ cup) white wine

25 g (1 oz) chopped flat-leaf (Italian) parsley

130 g (5 oz/1 cup) grated gruyère cheese

a few small sprigs of thyme

1   **Preheat the oven** to 180°C (350°F/Gas 4). Grease a 15 x 25 cm (6 x 10 inch) ovenproof dish with melted butter or oil. Heat half the oil in a large frying pan and add the zucchini and half the garlic. Cook, stirring, over low heat for about 8 minutes, or until just beginning to soften. Season well with salt, pepper and nutmeg. Spread evenly into the dish.

2   **Score a cross** in the top of each tomato, plunge them into boiling water for 20 seconds and then peel the skin away from the cross. Chop flesh roughly. Cook onion in the remaining oil over low heat for 5 minutes, stirring often. Add the remaining garlic, tomato, wine and parsley. Cook, stirring often, for about 10 minutes, or until all the liquid has evaporated.

3   **Sprinkle the cheese** over the zucchini and spread tomato mixture over the top. Scatter with sprigs of thyme and bake for 20 minutes, or until heated through.

LEEKS A LA GRECQUE

SERVES 4

60 ml (2 fl oz/¼ cup) olive oil
30 ml (1 fl oz) white wine
1 tablespoon tomato paste (concentrated purée)
¼ teaspoon sugar
1 bay leaf
1 sprig of thyme
1 garlic clove, crushed
4 coriander seeds, crushed
4 peppercorns
8 small leeks, trimmed
1 teaspoon lemon juice
1 tablespoon chopped parsley

1 Put the oil, wine, tomato paste, sugar, bay leaf, thyme, garlic, coriander, peppercorns and 250 ml (9 fl oz/1 cup) water in a large non-aluminium frying pan. Bring to the boil, cover and simmer for 5 minutes.

2 Add the leeks in a single layer and bring to simmering point. Reduce the heat, cover the pan again and cook for 20–30 minutes, or until the leeks are tender (pierce with a fine skewer). Lift out the leeks and put them in a serving dish.

3 Add the lemon juice to the cooking liquid and boil rapidly until the liquid is slightly syrupy. Remove the bay leaf, thyme and peppercorns. Season with salt and pour over the leeks. Serve the leeks cold, sprinkled with chopped parsley.

MUSHROOMS A LA GRECQUE

SERVES 4

2 tomatoes

80 ml (3 fl oz/⅓ cup) extra virgin olive oil

60 ml (2 fl oz/¼ cup) white wine

2 French shallots, finely chopped

1 garlic clove, crushed

6 coriander seeds, lightly crushed

1 bay leaf

1 sprig of thyme

500 g (1 lb 2 oz) button mushrooms

2 teaspoons lemon juice

pinch of sugar

1 tablespoon chopped parsley

1   Score a cross in the top of each tomato. Plunge tomatoes into boiling water for 20 seconds, then drain and peel the skin away from the cross. Chop the flesh, discarding the cores.

2   Place oil, wine, tomato, shallots, garlic, coriander seeds, bay leaf, thyme and 250 ml (9 fl oz/1 cup) water in a non-aluminium saucepan. Bring to the boil. Simmer, covered, for 10 minutes. Uncover pan, add mushrooms and simmer for a further 10 minutes, stirring occasionally. Lift the mushrooms out with a slotted spoon and put them in a serving dish.

3   Boil cooking liquid rapidly until you have only about 250 ml (9 fl oz/1 cup) left. Remove the bay leaf and thyme. Add the lemon juice and season with salt, pepper and the sugar. Pour the liquid over the mushrooms and leave to cool. Serve the mushrooms cold, sprinkled with chopped parsley.

CELERIAC REMOULADE

SERVES 4

juice of 1 lemon

2 celeriac, trimmed and peeled

2 tablespoons capers

5 cornichons, chopped

2 tablespoons finely chopped parsley

MUSTARD MAYONNAISE

2 egg yolks

1 tablespoon white wine vinegar or
  lemon juice

1 tablespoon dijon mustard

125 ml (4 fl oz/½ cup) light olive oil

1 Place 1 litre (35 fl oz/4 cups) cold water in a large bowl and add half the lemon juice. Roughly grate the celeriac and then place in the acidulated water to stop it from browning. Bring a saucepan of water to the boil and add the remaining lemon juice. Drain the celeriac and add to the water. After 1 minute, drain and cool under running water. Pat dry with paper towels.

2 To make the mayonnaise, put the egg yolks, vinegar or lemon juice and mustard in a bowl or food processor and whisk together. Add the oil, drop by drop from the tip of a teaspoon, whisking constantly until it begins to thicken, then add the oil in a very thin stream. (If using a processor, pour in the oil in a thin, steady stream with the motor running.) Season and, if necessary, thin with a little warm water.

3 Toss celeriac with mayonnaise, capers, cornichons and parsley. Serve with bread.

POTATO SALAD

SERVES 4

4 large waxy (all-purpose) potatoes, cubed

3 celery stalks

1 red capsicum (pepper)

1 tablespoon olive oil

80 ml (3 fl oz/⅓ cup) mayonnaise (recipe on page 156)

juice of 1 lemon

1½ tablespoons chopped parsley

1 **Put the potatoes** in a large saucepan, cover with cold water and cook for 15 minutes, or until just tender (don't let them overcook). Refresh under cold water and drain.

2 **String the celery stalks.** Cut stalks into very small dice. Cut the capsicum in half, remove the seeds and dice finely.

3 **Put the potato,** celery and capsicum in a bowl, add the olive oil, mayonnaise, lemon juice and parsley and toss well. Season well before serving.

ALIGOT

SERVES 4

800 g (1 lb 12 oz) boiling potatoes, cut into even-sized pieces

70 g (2 oz) butter

2 garlic cloves, crushed

3 tablespoons milk

300 g (11 oz) cantal (or mild cheddar cheese), grated

1 Cook potatoes in boiling salted water for 20–30 minutes, or until tender. Meanwhile, melt the butter in a small saucepan over low heat and add the garlic. Mash the potatoes and then sieve to give a really smooth purée (don't use a food processor or they will become gluey).

2 Return the potato purée to the pan over gentle heat and add the garlic butter and milk. Mix together well and then add the cheese, handful by handful. Beat in the cheese — once it has melted the mixture will be stretchy. Season with salt and pepper before serving.

DESSERTS & BAKING

COFFEE CRÉMETS WITH CHOCOLATE SAUCE

SERVES 4

250 g (9 oz) cream cheese

250 ml (9 fl oz/1 cup) thick (double/heavy) cream

4 tablespoons strong brewed coffee, cooled

80 g (3 oz/⅓ cup) caster (superfine) sugar

CHOCOLATE SAUCE

100 g (4 oz) dark chocolate

50 g (2 oz) unsalted butter

1   Line four 100 ml (4 oz) perforated ceramic ramekins or heart-shaped moulds with muslin (cheesecloth), leaving enough muslin hanging over the side to wrap over each dessert. Place the ramekins on a tray.

2   Beat **cream cheese** until smooth and whisk in the cream. Add the coffee and sugar and mix to combine. Then pour into the ramekins and fold the muslin over the top. Refrigerate for at least 1½ hours. Unwrap the muslin and turn the crémets out onto individual plates, carefully peeling the muslin off.

3   To make the chocolate sauce, gently melt chocolate in a saucepan with the butter and 4 tablespoons of water. Stir until combined well and the mixture is glossy. Allow to cool slightly, then pour a little chocolate sauce over each crémet and serve immediately.

PEARS IN RED WINE

SERVES 6

1 tablespoon arrowroot
750 ml (26 gl oz/3 cups) red wine
110 g (4 oz) sugar
1 stick cinnamon
6 cloves
1 tablespoon grated orange zest
1 tablespoons grated lemon zest
6 pears (ripe but still firm)

1 **Mix the arrowroot** with 2 tablespoons of the wine and set aside. Heat the remaining wine in a saucepan with the sugar, cinnamon stick, cloves and orange and lemon zest. Simmer gently for a few minutes, stirring occasionally, until the sugar has dissolved.

2 **Peel the pears,** but don't remove the stalks. Put the whole pears in the saucepan of wine and cover and poach gently for about 25 minutes, or until they are very tender, turning them occasionally. Lift them out with a slotted spoon and place on serving plates.

3 **Strain the wine mixture,** discarding solids, then pour back into the saucepan. Stir the arrowroot mixture and add to the hot wine. Simmer gently, stirring occasionally, until thickened. Pour over the pears and stand until cooled. Serve with cream.

PETITS POTS DE CRÈME

SERVES 4

400 ml (14 fl oz) milk

1 vanilla bean

3 egg yolks

1 egg

80 g (3 oz/⅓ cup) caster (superfine) sugar

1 Preheat the oven to 140°C (275°F/Gas 1). Put the milk in a saucepan. Split the vanilla bean in two, scrape out the seeds and add the seeds and scraped bean to the milk. Bring the milk just to the boil, then remove from the heat and let stand for 20 minutes to infuse.

2 Meanwhile, combine the egg yolks, egg and sugar. Strain the milk over the egg mixture and discard the vanilla bean. Stir well, then skim off the surface to remove any foam.

3 Using four 125 ml (4 fl oz/½ cup) ramekins, ladle in the mixture and place in a roasting tin. Pour hot water into the tin to come halfway up the sides of the ramekins. Bake for about 30 minutes, or until the custards are firm to the touch. Leave the ramekins on a wire rack to cool, then refrigerate until ready to serve.

CHOCOLATE MOUSSE

SERVES 8

300 g (11 oz) good quality dark
  chocolate, chopped

30 g (1 oz) unsalted butter, chopped

2 eggs, lightly beaten

3 tablespoons Cognac or brandy

4 egg whites

100 g (4 oz) caster (superfine) sugar

500 ml (17 fl oz/2 cups) thick (double/
  heavy) cream

1 Put the chocolate in a heatproof bowl and set over a saucepan of simmering water, making sure the base of the bowl doesn't touch the water or the chocolate will form into a hard, unusable clump. Leave the chocolate until it looks soft and then stir until smooth. Add the butter and stir until melted. Remove the bowl from the saucepan and cool the chocolate mixture for a few minutes. Add the lightly beaten eggs and Cognac and stir to combine well.

2 Beat the egg whites in a clean dry bowl until soft peaks form, gradually adding the sugar. Whisk one third of the egg whites into the chocolate mixture to loosen. Gently fold in the remaining egg whites with a large metal spoon or spatula.

3 Whip the cream using electric beaters until firm peaks form. Gently fold into the mousse. Pour into serving glasses, then cover and refrigerate for at least 4 hours.

CINNAMON BAVAROIS

SERVES 6

315 ml (11 fl oz/1¼ cups) milk

1 teaspoon ground cinnamon

55 g (2 oz/¼ cup) caster (superfine) sugar

3 egg yolks

3 gelatine leaves or 1½ teaspoons powdered gelatine

½ teaspoon natural vanilla extract

170 ml (6 fl oz/⅔ cup) thick (double/heavy) cream

cinnamon, for dusting

1 Put the milk, cinnamon and half the sugar in a saucepan and bring to the boil. Whisk the egg yolks and remaining sugar until light and fluffy. Whisk the boiling milk into the yolks, then pour back into the saucepan and cook, stirring, until it is thick enough to coat the back of a wooden spoon. Do not let it boil or the custard will split.

2 Soak the gelatine in cold water until soft, drain and add to the hot custard with the vanilla. If using powdered gelatine, sprinkle it on the hot custard, leave it to sponge for a minute, then stir it in. Strain the custard into a clean bowl and cool. Whip the cream and fold it into the custard. Pour mixture into six 125 ml (4 oz/½ cup) oiled bavarois moulds. Leave in the refrigerator to set.

3 Unmould bavarois by holding each mould in a hot cloth and inverting it onto a plate with a quick shake. Dust with the extra cinnamon.

VANILLA SOUFFLÉ WITH RASPBERRY COULIS

SERVES 6

40 g (1½ oz) butter

115 g (4 oz/½ cup) caster (superfine) sugar

250 ml (9 fl oz/1 cup) milk

1 teaspoon natural vanilla extract

1 vanilla bean, split lengthways

1 tablespoon plain (all-purpose) flour

4 eggs, separated

1 egg white

icing (confectioners') sugar, for dusting

RASPBERRY COULIS

400 g (14 oz) raspberries

80 g (3 oz) icing (confectioners') sugar

lemon juice to taste

1 Preheat the oven 190°C (375°F/Gas 5). Use a double layer of non-stick baking paper to wrap around six 250 ml (9 fl oz/1 cup) soufflé dishes, making sure that the paper extends 5 cm (2 inch) above the rim. Secure the collars firmly by tying with kitchen string.

2 Melt 20 g (¾ oz) of butter and grease the soufflé dishes. Sprinkle each with a little caster sugar and turn dishes to coat the entire surface. Turn over and tap to remove excess sugar.

3 Heat the milk, all but one tablespoon of the sugar, and the vanilla extract and vanilla bean in a small saucepan over low heat. Stir occasionally for 3–4 minutes, or until the sugar has dissolved. Remove from the heat and set aside.

4 Melt remaining butter in a saucepan over medium heat. Add the flour and stir to a smooth paste, then cook, stirring, for 1 minute. Remove from the heat and gradually whisk in the milk mixture. Return to the heat, stirring, until thick and smooth. Remove the vanilla bean and allow to cool.

5 Whisk the egg yolks, one at a time, into vanilla mixture until combined. Whisk the egg whites in a bowl until stiff peaks form. Gradually add remaining sugar, whisking continuously. Fold meringue into the milk mixture. Spoon into soufflé dishes. Run a spoon around the tops 2.5 cm (1 inch) from the edge.

6 Stand the soufflé dishes in a roasting tin, then pour in enough hot water to come halfway up the sides. Bake in the oven on the bottom shelf for 5 minutes. Reduce heat to 180°C (350°F/ Gas 4). Cook for a further 10–15 minutes, or until risen.

7 To make the coulis, blend or process the raspberries and sugar until a purée forms. Sieve mixture, discarding the solids. Add the lemon juice to taste. Dust the soufflés with icing sugar and serve with the coulis.

CRÈME BRÛLÉE

SERVES 8

500 ml (17 fl oz/2 cups) thick (double/ heavy) cream

200 ml (7 fl oz) milk

125 g (5 oz) caster (superfine) sugar

1 vanilla bean

5 egg yolks

1 egg white

1 tablespoon orange flower water

100 g (4 oz) raw (demerara) sugar

1   Preheat oven to 120°C (250°F/Gas ½). Put the cream, milk and half the caster sugar in a saucepan with the vanilla bean and bring just to the boil.

2   Combine remaining caster sugar, egg yolks and egg white. Strain the milk mixture over the egg mixture, whisking well. Stir in the orange flower water.

3   Pour into eight 125 ml (4 fl oz/½ cup) ramekins and place in a roasting tin. Pour the hot water into the tin to come halfway up the sides of the ramekins. Cook for 1½ hours, or until desserts are set in the centre. Allow to cool. Refrigerate until ready to serve. Just before serving, sprinkle the tops with raw sugar and caramelize under a hot grill (broiler) or with a chef's blowtorch.

CHOCOLATE SOUFFLÉS

SERVES 8

40 g (1½ oz) unsalted butter, softened

170 g (6 oz/¾ cup) caster (superfine) sugar

SOUFFLÉS

1 quantity crème pâtissière (page 155)

90 g (3 oz/¾ cup) unsweetened cocoa powder

3 tablespoons chocolate or coffee liqueur

85 g (3 oz) dark chocolate, chopped

12 egg whites

3 tablespoons caster (superfine) sugar

icing (confectioners') sugar

1 **To prepare the dishes**, brush insides of eight 310 ml (10 fl oz/1¼ cup) soufflé dishes with softened butter. Pour a little caster sugar into each one, turn the dishes round to coat thoroughly and then tip out any excess sugar. Preheat the oven to 190°C (375°F/Gas 5) and put a large baking tray in the oven to heat up.

2 **Warm the crème pâtissière** in a bowl over a saucepan of simmering water, then remove from the heat. Whisk the cocoa powder, chocolate liqueur and chocolate into the crème pâtissière.

3 **Beat the egg whites** in a clean dry bowl until firm peaks form. Whisk in the sugar gradually to make a stiff glossy mixture. Whisk half the egg white into the crème pâtissière to loosen it, and then fold in the remainder with a large metal spoon or spatula. Pour into the soufflé dishes and run

your thumb around the inside rim of each dish, 2.5 cm (1 inch) into the soufflé mixture to help the soufflés rise without sticking.

4 **Place dishes** on the hot baking tray and bake for about 15–18 minutes, or until soufflés are well risen and wobble slightly when tapped. Test with a skewer through a crack in the side of a soufflé—the skewer should come out clean or slightly moist. If it is slightly moist, by the time you get the soufflés to the table, they will be cooked in the centre. Serve immediately, dusted with a little icing sugar.

CRÈME CARAMEL

SERVES 6

650 ml (22½ fl oz) milk
1 vanilla bean
125 g (5 oz) caster (superfine) sugar
3 eggs, beaten
3 egg yolks

CARAMEL
100 g (4 oz) caster (superfine) sugar

1   **To make the caramel,** put the sugar in a heavy-based saucepan and heat until it dissolves and starts to caramelize — swirl the pan as the sugar cooks to keep the colouring even. Remove from the heat and add 2 tablespoons of water; take care as the mixture will spit. Pour into six 125 ml (4 fl oz) ramekins and allow to cool.

2   **Preheat oven to 180°C** (350°F/Gas 4). Put the milk and vanilla bean in a saucepan and bring just to the boil. Combine the sugar, eggs and egg yolks. Strain the boiling milk over the egg mixture. Stir well, then strain the custard. Ladle into the ramekins and place in a roasting tin. Pour enough hot water into the tin to come halfway up the sides of the ramekins. Cook for 35–40 minutes, or until firm to the touch. Remove from the tin and stand for 15 minutes. Unmould onto plates, pour on any leftover caramel and serve immediately.

CRÊPES SUZETTE

SERVES 6

250 g (9 oz/2 cups) plain (all-purpose) flour

pinch salt

1 teaspoon sugar

2 eggs, lightly beaten

400 ml (14 fl oz) milk

20 g (¾ oz) butter, melted

2 tablespoons grated orange zest

1 tablespoon grated lemon zest

butter or oil for frying

125 g (5 oz) caster (superfine) sugar

250 ml (9 fl oz/1 cup) orange juice

1 tablespoon grated orange zest

2 tablespoons brandy or Cognac

2 tablespoons Grand Marnier or other orange-flavoured liqueur

50 g (2 oz) unsalted butter, diced

1 Sift flour, salt and sugar into a bowl and make a well in the centre. Mix the eggs and milk with 100 ml (3½ fl oz) of water and pour slowly into the well, whisking until a smooth batter forms. Stir in the melted butter. Cover and refrigerate for 20 minutes. Stir the orange and lemon zest into crêpe batter.

2 Heat and lightly grease a crêpe pan. Pour in just enough batter to coat the base of the pan in a thin even layer, pouring out any excess. Cook over medium heat for about 1 minute, or until the crêpe starts to come away from the side of the pan.

3 Turn the crêpe and cook on the other side for 1 minute, or until light golden. Repeat with the remaining batter. Fold the crêpes into quarters.

4 Melt the sugar in a large frying pan over low heat and and cook to a caramel, tilting the pan so the caramel browns evenly. Pour in the orange juice and zest; boil for 2 minutes. Put the crêpes in the pan and spoon the sauce over them.

5 Add brandy and Grand Marnier and flambé by lighting the pan with your gas flame or a match (stand well back when you do this and keep a pan lid handy for emergencies). Add the butter and swirl the pan until it melts. Serve immediately.

CHERRY CLAFOUTIS

SERVES 6

200 ml (7 fl oz) thick (double/heavy) cream

1 vanilla bean

100 ml (4 fl oz) milk

3 eggs

50 g (2 oz) caster (superfine) sugar

70 g (2 oz) plain (all-purpose) flour

1 tablespoon kirsch

450 g (1 lb) black cherries

icing (confectioners') sugar, for dusting

1 Preheat the oven to 180°C (350°F/Gas 4). Put the cream in a small saucepan. Split vanilla bean in two, scrape out the seeds and add the scraped seeds and bean to the cream. Heat gently for a few minutes, then remove from the heat, add the milk and cool. Strain the mixture, discarding the vanilla bean.

2 Whisk the eggs with the sugar and flour, then stir into the cream mixture. Add the kirsch and cherries and stir well. Pour into a 23 cm (9 in) round baking dish and bake for about 30 minutes, or until golden on top. Dust with icing sugar just before serving. Serve warm.

PITHIVIERS

SERVES 6

140 g (5 oz) unsalted butter

140 g (5 oz) caster (superfine) sugar

2 beaten eggs

2 tablespoons dark rum

orange zest, finely grated

140 g (5 oz) ground almonds

20 g (1 oz) plain (all-purpose) flour

1 quantity puff pastry (see page 152)

1 beaten egg extra, for brushing

icing (confectioners') sugar, for dusting

1 **To make the filling,** beat butter and caster sugar until creamy. Mix in eggs, dark rum and the orange zest . Fold in ground almonds and flour. On a floured surface, roll out one half of the pastry.

2 **Cut out a 28 cm** (11 inch) circle of pastry and place on a baking tray lined with baking paper. Spread the filling over the pastry, leaving a 2 cm (¾ inch) border around the edges. Brush borders with the extra beaten egg. Roll out remaining pastry and cut out another 28 cm (11 inch) circle. Lay circle on top of the filling and press the edges of pastry together. Cover and refrigerate for 1 hour.

3 **Preheat the oven to 220°C** (425°F/Gas 7). Brush 1 beaten egg over the pithivier, then score the top with curved lines, in a spiral pattern. Bake for 25–30 minutes, or until pastry has risen and is golden brown. Dust with icing sugar and cool.

GÂTEAU BASQUE

SERVES 8

4 tablespoons thick black cherry or
plum jam

1 egg, lightly beaten

ALMOND PASTRY

400 g (14 oz) plain (all-purpose) flour

1 teaspoon finely grated lemon zest

50 g (2 oz) ground almonds

150 g (6 oz) caster (superfine) sugar

1 egg

1 egg yolk

¼ teaspoon natural vanilla extract

150 g (6 oz) unsalted butter, softened

ALMOND CRÈME PÂTISSIÈRE

6 egg yolks

200 g (7 oz) caster (superfine) sugar

60 g (2 oz) plain (all-purpose) flour

60 g (2 oz) ground almonds

1 litre (35 fl oz/4 cups) milk

2 vanilla beans

1 **To make pastry,** combine flour, lemon zest and almonds. Turn out onto a work surface; make a well in the centre. Put sugar, egg, egg yolk, vanilla extract and butter in the well.

2 **Combine the sugar,** eggs, vanilla extract and butter, using a pecking action with your fingertips and thumb. Use the edge of a palette knife to incorporate the flour, flicking it onto the dough and then chopping through it. Then bring the dough together with your hands. Cover with plastic wrap and refrigerate for at least 30 minutes.

3 **Roll out two-thirds** of the pastry on a lightly floured work surface to fit a 25 cm (10 inch) tart tin. Trim the edge and chill in the fridge for a further 30 minutes. Preheat oven to 180°C (350°F/Gas 4).

4 **To make almond crème pâtissière,** whisk together the egg yolks and sugar until pale and creamy. Sift in the flour

and ground almonds and combine thoroughly. Put the milk in a saucepan. Split the vanilla beans in two, scrape out the seeds and add the scraped seeds and bean to the milk. Bring just to the boil and then strain over the egg yolk mixture, stirring continuously to combine well. Return mixture to the clean saucepan and bring slowly to the boil, stirring constantly until smooth. Boil for 2 minutes, then allow to cool.

5 **Spread the jam** over the base of the pastry case, then spread with the crème pâtissière. Roll out remaining pastry to make a top for the pie. Brush the edge of the pastry case with beaten egg, put the pastry top over it and press together around the side. Trim the edge. Brush the top with beaten egg and score in a crisscross pattern. Bake for 40 minutes, or until golden brown. Cool for at least 30 minutes before serving.

ÎLE FLOTTANTE

SERVES 6

MERINGUE

4 egg whites

125 g (5 oz/½ cup) caster (superfine)
sugar

¼ teaspoon natural vanilla extract

PRALINE

55 g (2 oz/¼ cup) sugar

55 g (2 oz) flaked almonds

2 quantities crème anglaise (page 155)

1 Preheat oven to 140°C (275°F/Gas 1). Put the roasting tin in the oven to heat up. Grease and line the base of a 1.5 litre 51 fl oz/6 cup) charlotte mould with a circle of baking paper and lightly grease the base and side.

2 To make the meringue, beat the egg whites in a clean dry bowl until very stiff peaks form. Whisk in the sugar gradually to make a very stiff glossy meringue. Whisk in the vanilla extract.

3 Spoon the meringue into the mould, smooth the surface and place a greased circle of baking paper on top. Put mould into the hot roasting tin and pour boiling water into tin until it comes halfway up the side of the charlotte mould.

4 Bake for 50–60 minutes, or until a knife poked into the centre of the meringue comes out clean. Remove the circle of paper, put a plate over the meringue and turn it over. Lift off the mould and the other circle of paper and leave to cool.

5 To make the praline, grease a sheet of foil and lay it out flat on the work surface. Put sugar in a small saucepan with 3 tablespoons water and heat gently until sugar is completely dissolved. Bring to the boil and cook until deep golden, then quickly tip in the flaked almonds and pour onto the oiled foil. Spread out a little and leave to cool. When the praline has hardened, grind it to a fine powder in a food processor or with a mortar and pestle.

6 Sprinkle the praline over the meringue and pour a sea of warmed crème anglaise around its base (the name of this recipe means floating island). Serve in wedges with the remaining crème anglaise.

PARIS-BREST

SERVES 6

1 quantity choux pastry (page 153)
1 egg, lightly beaten
1 tablespoon flaked almonds
1 quantity crème pâtissière (page 155)
icing (confectioners') sugar, for dusting

PRALINE

115 g (4 oz/½ cup) caster (superfine) sugar
90 g (3 oz/1 cup) flaked almonds

1   **Preheat the oven to 200°C** (400°F/Gas 6) and put the choux pastry in a piping bag fitted with a wide nozzle (about 2 cm/¾ inch wide). Draw a 20 cm (8 inch) circle on the back of a piece of baking paper in a dark pen so that the circle shows through onto the other side. Put the paper on a baking tray, pen-side down.

2   **Pipe a ring of pastry** over the guide you have drawn. Now pipe another ring of pastry directly inside this one so that you have one thick ring. Pipe another two circles on top of the first two and continue until you have used all of the choux pastry. Brush the choux ring with beaten egg and sprinkle with the flaked almonds.

3   **Bake choux ring** for 20–30 minutes, then reduce the oven to 180°C (350°F/Gas 4) and bake for a further 20–25 minutes. Remove from the baking tray and place on a wire rack

4   **Immediately slice ring in half** horizontally, making the base twice as deep as the top. Lift off the top and scoop out any uncooked pastry from the base. Leave to cool completely.

5   **To make praline,** grease a sheet of baking foil and lay it out flat on the work surface. Put the sugar in a small saucepan with 125 ml (4 fl oz/2 cup) water and heat gently until sugar is completely dissolved. Bring to the boil and cook until deep golden, then quickly tip in the flaked almonds and pour onto the oiled foil. Spread a little and leave to cool. When the praline has hardened, grind it to a fine powder in a food processor or with a mortar and pestle. Mix into the cold crème pâtissière.

6   **Spoon crème pâtissière** into the base of the choux pastry ring and cover with the top. Dust with icing sugar to serve.

CHOCOLATE-HAZELNUT CAKE

SERVES 10–12

150 g (6 oz), chopped unsalted butter

175 g (6 oz) dark chocolate, chopped

8 eggs, separated

200 g (7 oz) caster (superfine) sugar

1 teaspoon vanilla extract

40 g (1½ oz/⅓ cup) unsweetened cocoa powder, sifted

250 g (9 oz/2 cups) ground hazelnut

GANACHE

250 ml (9 fl oz/1 cup) thick (double/heavy) cream

200 g (7 oz) dark chocolate, chopped

1 Preheat the oven to 180°C (350°F/Gas 4). Lightly grease and flour a 24 cm (9½ inch) spring-form pan.

2 Combine butter and chocolate in a bowl and set over a saucepan of simmering water, making sure the base of the bowl doesn't touch the water. Stir until melted. Remove from the heat and stir until smooth and well combined. Allow to cool slightly.

3 Combine egg yolks, sugar and vanilla in a bowl. Using electric beaters, whisk until mixture is thick and pale. Add the chocolate mixture and stir until smooth. Add the cocoa and ground hazelnuts and stir until well combined.

4 Whisk egg whites in a large bowl until firm peaks form. Stir a quarter of the egg whites into the chocolate mixture. Gently fold in the remaining egg whites until well combined.

5 Pour mixture into the prepared pan and bake for 1 hour, until firm to touch. Allow to cool in the pan for 15 minutes, then turn out onto a wire rack to cool completely.

6 To make the ganache, put the cream in a saucepan and bring to the boil. Put chocolate in a bowl and add the cream. Stir until the chocolate is melted and the mixture is smooth. Refrigerate the ganache until cooled and beginning to thicken. Whisk until ganache thickens slightly. Spread over cooled cake.

Note: This cake can be stored in an airtight container in the refrigerator for up to three days.

APPLE TART

SERVES 8

1 quantity sweet pastry (page 151)

½ quantity crème pâtissière (page 155)

4 dessert apples

80 g (3 oz/¼ cup) apricot jam (jelly)

1 **Preheat oven to 180°C** (350°F/Gas 4). Roll out the pastry to line a 23 cm (9 inch) round loose-based fluted tart tin. Chill for 20 minutes.

2 **Line the pastry shell** with a crumpled piece of baking paper and baking beads (use dried beans or rice if you don't have beads). Blind bake the pastry for 10 minutes, remove the paper and beads and bake for a further 3–5 minutes, or until the pastry is just cooked but still very pale.

3 **Fill the pastry** with crème pâtissière. Peel and core the apples, cut them in half and then into thin slices. Arrange over the top of the tart. Bake for 25–30 minutes or until the apples are golden and the pastry is cooked. Leave to cool completely, then melt jam with 1 tablespoon water, sieve out any lumps and brush over the apples to make them shine.

SERVES 8

SWEET PASTRY

350 g (12 oz) plain (all-purpose) flour

small pinch salt

150 g (6 oz) unsalted butter, chopped

100 g (4 oz) icing (confectioners') sugar

2 eggs, beaten

FILLING

4 eggs

2 egg yolks

275 g (10 oz) caster (superfine) sugar

190 ml (6 fl oz) thick (double/heavy) cream

275 ml (9½ fl oz) lemon juice

3 tablespoons finely grated lemon zest

1 Sift the flour and salt onto a work surface and make a well in the centre. Put the butter into the well and work, using a pecking action with your fingertips and thumb, until it is very soft. Add the sugar and combine. Add the eggs and combine. Gradually incorporate flour, flicking it onto the butter mixture and then chopping through it until you have a rough dough. Bring mixture together with your hands and then knead a few times to make a smooth dough. Roll into a ball, cover with plastic wrap and refrigerate for 1 hour.

2 Preheat oven to 190°C (375°F/Gas 5). Roll out pastry on a lightly floured surface to line a 23 cm (9 inch) round loose-based fluted tart tin. Refrigerate for 20 minutes.

3 To make the filling, whisk together the eggs, egg yolks and sugar. Add the cream, whisking constantly, then add the lemon juice and zest and whisk to combine well.

4 Line the pastry shell with a crumpled piece of baking paper and baking beads (use dried beans or rice if you don't have beads). Blind bake the pastry for 10 minutes, remove the paper and beads and bake for a further 3–5 minutes, or until the pastry is just cooked but still very pale. Remove from the oven and reduce the temperature to 150°C (300°F/Gas 2).

5 Put the tin on a baking tray and carefully pour the filling into the pastry case. Return to the oven for 35–40 minutes, or until the filling has set. Cool completely before serving.

PEAR AND ALMOND TART

SERVES 8

1 quantity sweet pastry (page 151)

55 g (2 oz/¼ cup) caster (superfine) sugar

1 vanilla pod

3 pears (ripe but still firm), peeled, halved and cored

3 tablespoons apricot jam (jelly)

ALMOND FILLING

150 g (6 oz) unsalted butter, softened

145 g (5 oz/⅔ cup) caster (superfine) sugar

few drops of natural vanilla extract

2 large eggs, lightly beaten

140 g (5 oz/1⅓ cups) ground almonds

finely grated zest of 1 small lemon

30 g (1 oz/¼ cup) plain (all-purpose) flour

1 Preheat the oven to 190°C (375°F/Gas 5). Roll out pastry to line a 23 cm (9 inch) round loose-based fluted tart tin. Chill for 20 minutes.

2 Put the sugar and vanilla pod in a saucepan. Add pears and pour in just enough water to cover them, then remove the pears. Bring the water to a simmer and simmer liquid for 5 minutes. Add the pears, cover and poach for 5–10 minutes until tender. Drain and leave to cool.

3 To make almond filling, beat the butter, sugar and vanilla extract together until pale and creamy. Beat in eggs gradually and then fold in the almonds, lemon zest and flour.

4 Line the pastry shell with a crumpled piece of baking paper and baking beads (use dried beans or rice if you don't have beads). Blind bake the pastry for 10 minutes, remove the paper and beads and bake for a further 3–5 minutes, or until the pastry is just cooked but still very pale. Reduce the oven temperature to 180°C (350°F/Gas 4).

5 Spread three-quarters of the filling in the pastry shell and put the pear halves on top, cut side down and stalk ends in the middle. Fill gaps with remaining filling, then bake for about 35 minutes, or until the filling is golden and firm. Melt the jam with 1 teaspoon water, sieve out any lumps and brush over the pears to make them shine.

MIXED BERRY TARTLETS

1 quantity sweet pastry (page 151)

FRANGIPANE
250 g (9 oz) unsalted butter, softened

250 g (9 oz/2 cups) icing sugar

250 g (9 oz/2½ cups) ground almonds

40 g (1½ oz/⅓ cup) plain flour

5 eggs, lightly beaten

400 g (14 oz) mixed berries

3 tablespoons apricot jam (jelly)

1   To make the frangipane, beat the butter until soft. Add the icing sugar, almonds and flour and beat well. Add the egg gradually, beating well. Put in a clean bowl, cover with plastic wrap and refrigerate for up to 24 hours.

2   Preheat the oven to 180°C (350°F/Gas 4). Roll out the pastry to a thickness of 2 mm (⅛ inch) and use to line ten 8 cm (3 inch) wide tartlet tins. Put the frangipane in a piping bag and pipe into the tartlet tins. Put the tins on a baking tray and bake for 10–12 minutes, or until golden.

3   Cool slightly on a wire rack, then arrange the berries on top. Melt the jam with 1 teaspoon water, sieve out any lumps and brush over the berries to make them shine.

APPLES AND PEARS IN PASTRY

SERVES 4

PASTRY

150 g (6 oz) unsalted butter

220 g (8 oz/1¾ cups) plain (all-purpose) flour

30 g (1 oz) caster (superfine) sugar

1 egg yolk

HAZELNUT FILLING

30 g (1 oz) hazelnuts, finely chopped

60 g (2 oz) unsalted butter, softened

80 g (3 oz/⅓ cup) soft brown sugar

pinch of mixed spice

2 dessert apples

2 pears (ripe but still firm)

juice of 1 lemon

1 egg, lightly beaten

1 To make the pastry, rub the butter into the flour until the mixture resembles fine breadcrumbs. Stir in the sugar. Add the egg yolk and 40–50 ml (2–2½ tablespoons) water and stir with a knife to form a dough. Turn out and bring together with your hands. Wrap in plastic wrap and refrigerate for at least 30 minutes. Preheat the oven to 200°C (400°F/Gas 6) and preheat the grill (broiler).

2 To make the hazelnut filling, toast the hazelnuts under the hot grill (broiler) for 1–2 minutes or until browned, then cool. Mix the softened butter with the sugar, hazelnuts and mixed spice. Peel and core the apples and pears, leaving the stalks and trimming the bases of the pears if they are very big. Roll in the lemon juice and stuff with the hazelnut filling.

3 Roll out the pastry to make a 32 cm (13 in) square, trimming off any untidy edges. Cut into four equal squares and place an apple or pear in the centre of each. Brush the edges of the pastry with water and then bring them up so that the corners of each pastry square meet at the top of the fruit. Press the edges together so that the pastry follows the curve of the fruit.

4 Cut off the excess pastry and crimp the edges to seal the fruit parcels thoroughly. Use the pastry trimmings to cut out leaves, then stick these onto the fruit by brushing the backs with water.

5 Brush the pastry fruits with the beaten egg to glaze and bake on a lightly greased baking tray for 35–40 minutes or until the pastry is cooked and browned. Serve with cream.

THE PERFECT TARTE TATIN

SERVES 8

215 g (8 oz/1¾ cups) plain (all-purpose) flour
160 g (6 oz) butter, chilled, chopped
1 egg yolk
1.3 kg (3 lb) apples
60 g (2 oz) unsalted butter
170 g (6 oz/¾ cups) caster (superfine) sugar
salt
whipped cream, to serve

1 To make the pastry, sift the flour and a pinch of salt into a large bowl, then rub the butter in until mixture resembles breadcrumbs. Add egg yolk and 2–3 teaspoons of ice-cold water and, using a flat-bladed knife, mix until dough just starts to come together. Turn out onto a work surface and push dough together with your hands, form into a disc then wrap in plastic wrap and refrigerate for 30 minutes.

2 Peel, core and quarter the apples. Combine butter and sugar in a deep, 25 cm (10 inch) ovenproof frying pan. Heat until butter is melted and sugar has dissolved. Arrange apples over the base of the pan, placing them in rings and making sure there are no gaps. Cook over low heat for 35–40 minutes, basting often with pan juices, or until the apples are soft and the pan juices are very reduced and are light caramel. Remove from heat. Preheat the oven to 190°C (375°F/Gas 5).

3 Roll out the pastry on a lightly floured board to form a 3 mm (⅛ inch) thick circle slightly larger than the frying pan. Lay pastry over the apples, pressing gently around the edge of the pan to enclose the apples. Trim the edge of pastry, then fold the trimmed edge back on itself to form a neat edge.

4 Bake for 25–30 minutes, or until pastry is golden and cooked through. Remove from the oven. Leave for 5 minutes before inverting the tart onto a plate. Serve the tart warm or at room temperature, with whipped cream.

STRAWBERRY MILLEFEUILLE

SERVES 6

1 quantity puff pastry (page 152)

5 tablespoons sugar

½ quantity crème pâtissière (page 155)

125 ml (4 fl oz/½ cup) thick (double/ heavy) cream

300 g (11 oz) strawberries, cut into quarters

icing (confectioners') sugar, for dusting

1 Preheat the oven to 180°C (350°F/Gas 4). Roll out the puff pastry on a lightly floured surface into a rectangle about 2 mm (⅛ inch) thick. Roll pastry around a rolling pin, then unroll it onto a baking tray lined with baking paper. Leave in the fridge for 15 minutes.

2 To make syrup, put the sugar and 185 ml (6 fl oz/¾ cup) water in a saucepan. Boil for 5 minutes; remove from the heat.

3 Cut out three 30 x 13 cm (12 x 5 inch) rectangles from the pastry. Place on a large baking tray. Prick with a fork, then cover with a sheet of baking paper and place a second baking tray on top to prevent pastry rising unevenly. Bake for 6 minutes, then remove the top baking tray and baking paper. Brush pastry with the syrup and bake for 6 minutes or until golden on top. Cool on a wire rack.

4 Whisk the crème pâtissière. Whip the cream and fold into the crème pâtissière. Spread half of this over one pastry rectangle and top with half of the strawberries. Place a second layer of pastry on top and spread with the remaining cream and strawberries. Cover with the last layer of pastry and dust with icing sugar, to serve.

RASPBERRY SOUFFLÉ

SERVES 6

40 g (1½ oz) unsalted butter, softened

170 g (6 oz/¾ cup) caster (superfine) sugar

SOUFFLÉ

½ quantity crème pâtissière (page 155)

400 g (14 oz) raspberries

3 tablespoons caster (superfine) sugar

8 egg whites

icing (confectioners') sugar, for dusting

1 **To prepare the soufflé dish,** brush the inside of a 1.5 litre (51 fl oz/6 cup) soufflé dish with the softened butter. Pour in the caster sugar, turn the dish round to coat thoroughly and then tip out any excess sugar. Preheat oven to 190°C (375°F/ Gas 5) and put a baking tray in the oven to heat up.

2 **Warm the crème pâtissière** in a bowl over a saucepan of simmering water, then remove from the heat. Put raspberries and half the sugar in a blender or food processor and mix until puréed (or mix by hand). Pass through a fine nylon sieve to get rid of the seeds. Add the crème pâtissière to the raspberries and whisk together.

3 **Beat the egg whites** in a clean, dry bowl until firm peaks forms. Whisk in the remaining sugar gradually to make a stiff glossy mixture. Whisk half the egg white into the raspberry mixture to loosen it, then fold in the remainder with a large metal spoon or spatula. Pour mixture into the soufflé dish and then run your thumb around the inside rim of the dish, about 2 cm (¾ inch) into the soufflé mixture, to help the soufflé rise without sticking.

4 **Put the dish** on the hot baking tray and bake for about 10 minutes, or until the soufflé is well risen and wobbles slightly when tapped. Test with a skewer through a crack in the side of the soufflé — the skewer should come out clean or slightly moist. If it is slightly moist, by the time you get the soufflé to the table, it will be cooked in the centre. Serve immediately, dusted with a little icing sugar.

TUILES

MAKES 12

2 egg whites

55 g (2 oz/¼ cup) caster (superfine)
  sugar

15 g (½ oz) plain (all-purpose) flour

55 g (2 oz/½ cup) ground almonds

2 teaspoons peanut oil

1   Beat the egg whites in a clean dry bowl until slightly
frothy. Mix in the sugar, then the flour, ground almonds and
oil. Preheat the oven to 200°C (400°F/Gas 6).

2   Line a baking tray with baking paper. Place one heaped
teaspoon of mixture on the tray and use the back of the spoon
to spread it into a thin round. Cover the tray with tuiles, leaving
2 cm (¾ inch) between them for spreading during cooking.

3   Bake for 5–6 minutes or until lightly golden. Lift the tuiles
off the tray with a metal spatula and drape over a rolling pin
while still warm to make them curl (you can use bottles and
glasses as well). Cool while you cook the rest of the tuiles.
Serve with ice creams and other creamy desserts.

MADELEINES

MAKES 14 (OR 30 SMALL ONES)

3 eggs

115 g (4 oz/½ cup) caster (superfine) sugar

155 g (6 oz/1¼ cups) plain (all-purpose) flour

100 g (4 oz) unsalted butter, melted

grated zest of 1 lemon and 1 orange

1 **Preheat the oven to 200°C** (400°F/Gas 6). Brush a tray of madeleine moulds with melted butter and coat with flour, then tap the tray to remove the excess flour.

2 **Whisk the eggs and sugar** until the mixture is thick and pale and the whisk leaves a trail when lifted. Gently fold in the flour, then the melted butter and grated lemon and orange zest. Spoon into the moulds, leaving a little room for rising. Bake for 12 minutes (small madeleines will need 7 minutes), or until very lightly golden and springy to the touch. Remove from the tray and cool on a wire rack.

PEACHES CARDINAL

SERVES 4

4 large ripe peaches

300 g (11 oz) raspberries

2 dessertspoons icing (confectioners') sugar, plus extra for dusting

1 **If the peaches are very ripe,** put them in a bowl and pour boiling water over them. Leave for a minute, then drain and carefully peel away the skin. If the fruit you have is not so ripe, dissolve 2 tablespoons sugar in a saucepan of water, add the peaches and cover the pan. Gently poach the peaches for 5–10 minutes, or until they are tender. Drain and peel.

2 **Let peaches cool** and then halve each one and remove the stone. Put two halves in each serving glass. Put raspberries in a food processor or blender and mix until puréed (or mix by hand). Pass through a fine nylon sieve to get rid of the seeds.

3 **Sift the icing sugar** over the raspberry purée and stir in. Drizzle the purée over the peaches, cover and chill thoroughly. Dust a little icing sugar over the top to serve.

CARAMEL ICE CREAM

SERVES 4

60 g (2 oz/¼ cup) sugar
80 ml (3 fl oz/⅓ cup) cream
3 egg yolks
330 ml (12 fl oz/1⅓ cups) milk
1 vanilla pod

1 **To make the caramel,** put 45 g (1½ oz) of the sugar in a heavy-based saucepan and heat until it dissolves and starts to caramelize — tip the saucepan from side to side as the sugar cooks to keep the colouring even. Remove from the heat and carefully add the cream (it will splutter). Stir over low heat until the caramel melts again.

2 **Whisk the egg yolks** and remaining sugar until light and fluffy. Put the milk and vanilla pod in a saucepan and bring just to the boil, then strain over the caramel. Bring back to the boil and pour over the egg yolk mixture, whisking continuously.

3 **Pour custard back** into the saucepan and cook, stirring, until it is thick enough to coat the back of a wooden spoon. Do not let it boil or the custard will split. Pass through a sieve into a bowl and leave over ice to cool quickly.

4 **Churn in an ice-cream maker,** following manufacturer's instructions. Alternatively, pour into a plastic freezer box, cover and freeze. Stir every 30 minutes with a whisk during freezing to break up the ice crystals and give a better texture. Freeze overnight with a layer of plastic wrap over the surface and the lid on the container. Allow to soften a little before serving.

BASICS

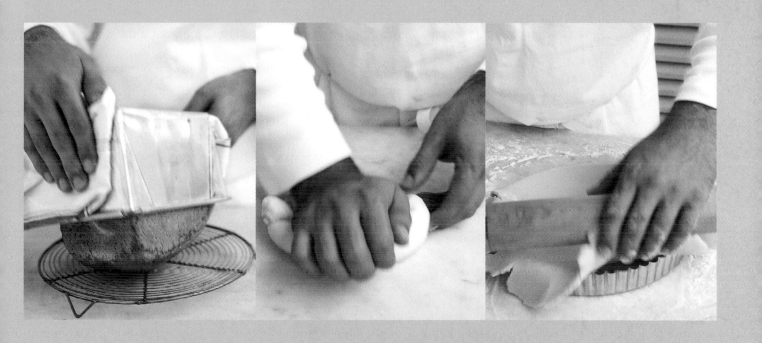

BRIOCHE

MAKES 1 LOAF

2 teaspoons dried yeast or 15 g (½ oz)
   fresh yeast

60 ml (2 fl oz/¼ cup) warm milk

2 tablespoons caster (superfine) sugar

220 g (8 oz/1¾ cups) plain (all-purpose)
   flour

pinch of salt

2 large eggs, lightly beaten

few drops natural vanilla extract

75 g (3 oz) butter, cubed

lightly beaten egg, to glaze

1 Mix the yeast with the warm milk and 1 teaspoon of the sugar. Leave for 10 minutes in a warm place until the yeast becomes frothy. If the yeast does not bubble and foam in this time, throw it away and start again.

2 Sift the flour into a large bowl and sprinkle with the salt and the rest of the sugar. Make a well in the centre and add eggs, vanilla extract and yeast mixture. Use a wooden spoon to mix all the ingredients together, then use your hands to knead the dough for 1 minute to bring it together. Transfer to a lightly floured work surface and gradually knead in the butter, piece by piece. Knead for 5 minutes, then put the dough into a clean bowl and cover with oiled plastic wrap. Leave to rise in a draught-free spot for 1–1½ hours or until the dough has doubled in size.

3 Knock back the dough by punching it with your fist several times to expel the air, and then lightly knead it again for a couple of minutes. Shape the dough into a rectangle and place in a 20 x 7 x 9 cm (8 x 2¾ x 3½ inch) buttered loaf tin. Cover with oiled plastic wrap and leave to rise in a draught-free spot for 30–35 minutes, or until risen almost to the top of the tin. Preheat the oven to 200°C (400°F/Gas 6).

4 Once brioche has risen, use scissors to carefully snip into the top of the dough at regular intervals. Snip three times on each side and twice at each end. Cuts should be about 2.5 cm (1 inch) deep. Brush top with egg and bake for 30–35 minutes, or until the top is a rich brown. Turn out of the tin and tap the bottom of the loaf — if it sounds hollow, it is cooked. Put it back in the tin upside down. Return to the oven for 5 minutes to crisp the base. Transfer to a wire rack and leave to cool.

MAKES 1 LOAF

2 teaspoons dried yeast or 15 g (½ oz) fresh yeast
250 g (9 oz/2 cups) strong plain (all-purpose) flour
½ teaspoon salt
3 tablespoons olive oil

1 **Mix the yeast** with 125 ml (4 fl oz/½ cup) warm water. Leave for 10 minutes in a warm place until the yeast becomes frothy. If yeast does not bubble and foam in this time, throw it away and start again.

2 **Sift the flour** into a large bowl and add the salt, olive oil and the yeast mixture. Mix until the dough clumps together and forms a ball.

3 **Turn dough out** onto a lightly floured work surface. Knead dough, adding a little more flour or a few drops of warm water if necessary, until you have a soft dough that is not sticky but is dry to the touch. Knead for 10 minutes, or until smooth, and the impression made by a finger springs back immediately.

4 **Rub the inside of a large bowl** with olive oil. Roll the ball of dough around in the bowl to coat it with oil. Cut a shallow cross on the top of the ball with a sharp knife. Leave dough in the bowl, cover with a tea (dish) towel or put in a plastic bag and leave in a draught-free spot for 1–1½ hours or until the dough has doubled in size. (Or, leave in the fridge for 8 hours to rise slowly).

5 **Knock back the dough** by punching it several times to expel the air and then knead it again for a couple of minutes. (At this stage the dough can be stored in the fridge for 4 hours, or frozen. Bring back to room temperature before continuing.) Leave in a warm place to double in size. Place in a tin, on a baking tray or use as directed in the recipe, then bake at 230°C (450°F/Gas 8) for 30 minutes. When cooked, the base of the bread will sound hollow when tapped.

TART PASTRY

MAKES 450 G (1 LB)

220 g (8 oz/1¾ cups) plain (all-purpose) flour

pinch of salt

150 g (6 oz) unsalted butter, chilled and diced

1 egg yolk

1 Sift the flour and salt into a large bowl, add the butter and rub in with your fingertips until the mixture resembles breadcrumbs. Add the egg yolk and a little cold water (about 2–3 teaspoons) and mix with the blade of a palette knife until the dough just starts to come together. Bring dough together with your hands and shape into a ball. Wrap in plastic wrap and put in the fridge to rest for at least 30 minutes. (You can make the dough in a food processor, using the pulse button.)

2 Roll out the pastry into a circle on a lightly floured surface and use to line a tart tin, as directed in the recipe. Trim the edge and pinch up the pastry edge to make an even border raised slightly above the rim of the tin. Slide onto a baking tray and rest in the fridge for 10 minutes.

SWEET PASTRY

MAKES 700 G (1 LB 9 OZ)

340 g (12 oz/2¾ cups) plain (all-purpose) flour
small pinch of salt
150 g (6 oz) unsalted butter
90 g (3 oz/¾ cup) icing (confectioners') sugar
2 eggs, beaten

1 **Sift flour and salt** onto a work surface and make a well in the centre. Put the butter into the well and work, using a pecking action with your fingertips and thumb, until it is very soft. Add the sugar to the butter and mix together. Add the eggs to the butter and mix together.

2 **Gradually incorporate the flour,** flicking it onto the mixture and then chopping through it until you have a rough dough. Bring together with your hands and then knead a few times to make a smooth dough. Roll into a ball, wrap in plastic wrap and put in the fridge for at least 1 hour.

3 **Roll out the pastry** into a circle on a lightly floured surface and use to line a tart tin, as directed in the recipe. Trim the edge and pinch up the pastry edge to make an even border raised slightly above the rim of the tin. Slide onto a baking tray and rest in the fridge for 10 minutes.

PUFF PASTRY

MAKES 650 G (1 LB 7 OZ)

250 g (9 oz/2 cups) plain (all-purpose) flour

1 teaspoon lemon juice

1 teaspoon salt

25 g (1 oz) butter, melted

200 g (7 oz) butter, chilled

1 **Sift the flour into a bowl** and make a well in the centre. Pour in 125 ml (4 fl oz/½ cup) water, the lemon juice, salt and melted butter. Draw in the flour with your fingertips, little by little, until you have a rough dough. Turn it out onto a work surface and knead with the heel of your hand until the dough is smooth. Shape into a ball and cut a cross on the top. Wrap with plastic wrap and refrigerate for 1–2 hours.

2 **Place the chilled butter** between two pieces of baking paper and beat with a rolling pin to make a square 1–2 cm (½–¾ inch) thick. Keep butter cool so that it doesn't harden again or melt further — it needs to be the same softness as the pastry or it will break up when you roll it.

3 **On a lightly floured surface,** roll out the dough in four different directions to form a cross large enough to hold the square of butter in its centre. Put the butter in the centre and

fold the four arms of dough over it, one by one, to enclose the butter completely. Position the dough so that it looks like a book with the spine to the left and the open piece of dough to the right. Roll the pastry away from you into a rectangle, keeping the corners as square as you can, then fold the top third down and the bottom third up to make a parcel of three even layers. Turn the pastry 90 degrees to the right and repeat the rolling, folding and turning, trying to keep the corners neat and square — this will help make the pastry layers even. Wrap in plastic wrap and chill for 30 minutes. (Mark the pastry with finger indents each time you refrigerate so you remember how many turns you have made.)

4 **Reposition as before,** the hinge to your left, then roll out, fold, turn and chill twice more. Rest for 30 minutes, then make two more turns as before. The pastry is ready to use.

CHOUX PASTRY

MAKES 500 G (1 LB 2 OZ)

150 g (6 oz) unsalted butter

220 g (8 oz/1¾ cups) plain (all-purpose)
flour, sifted twice

7 eggs

1 tablespoon caster (superfine) sugar

1 Melt the butter with 375 ml (13 fl oz/1½ cups) water in a saucepan, (13 fl oz/1hen bring it to a rolling boil. Remove from the heat and add all the flour at once and a pinch of salt. Return to the heat and beat continuously with a wooden spoon to make a smooth shiny paste that comes away from the side of the pan. Cool for a few minutes.

2 Beat in the eggs one at a time, until shiny and smooth — the mixture should drop off the spoon but not be too runny. Beat in the sugar. Store in a pastry bag in the fridge for up to 2 days.

CRÊPES

MAKES 12 SMALL OR 6 LARGE CRÊPES

250 g (9 oz/2 cups) plain (all-purpose) flour

pinch of salt

1 teaspoon sugar

2 eggs, lightly beaten

410 ml (14 fl oz/1²⁄₃ cups) milk

1 tablespoon melted butter

butter or oil, for frying

1 Sift the flour, salt and sugar into a bowl and make a well in the centre. Mix the eggs and milk together with 125 ml (4 fl oz/½ cup) water and pour slowly into the well, whisking all the time to incorporate the flour until you have a smooth batter. Stir in the melted butter. Cover and refrigerate for 20 minutes.

2 Heat a crêpe pan or a deep non-stick frying pan and grease with a little butter or oil. Pour in enough batter to coat the base of the pan in a thin even layer and tip out any excess. Cook over moderate heat for about a minute, or until the crêpe starts to come away from the side of the pan. Turn the crêpe and cook on the other side for 1 minute, or until lightly golden. Stack the crêpes on a plate with pieces of greaseproof paper between them and cover with foil while you cook the rest of the batter.

CRÈME PÂTISSIÈRE & CRÈME ANGLAISE

CRÈME PÂTISSIÈRE
MAKES 500 G (1 LB 2 OZ)

6 egg yolks

115 g (4 oz/½ cup) caster (superfine) sugar

30 g (1 oz/¼ cup) cornflour (cornstarch)

10 g (½ oz) plain (all-purpose) flour

560 ml (19 fl oz/2¼ cups) milk

1 vanilla pod

15 g (½ oz) butter

CRÈME ANGLAISE
MAKES 310 ML (11 FL OZ/1¼ CUPS)

310 ml (11 fl oz/1¼ cups) milk

1 vanilla pod

2 egg yolks

2 tablespoons caster (superfine) sugar

1 For the crème pâtissière, whisk together the egg yolks and half the sugar until pale and creamy. Sift in the cornflour and flour and mix together well.s

2 Put the milk, remaining sugar and the vanilla pod in a saucepan. Bring just to the boil and then strain over the egg yolk mixture, stirring continuously. Pour back into a clean saucepan and bring to the boil, stirring constantly — it will be lumpy at first but will become smooth as you stir. Boil for 2 minutes, then stir in the butter and leave to cool. Transfer to a bowl, lay plastic wrap on the surface to prevent a skin forming and refrigerate for up to 2 days.

3 For the crème anglaise, put milk in a saucepan. Split the vanilla pod in two, scrape out the seeds and add the whole lot to the milk. (This will give small black spots in the custard — if you don't want them, you can leave the vanilla pod whole.) Bring just to the boil. Whisk egg yolks and sugar until light and fluffy. Strain milk over the egg mixture, whisking continuously.

4 Pour custard back into the saucepan and cook, stirring, until it is thick enough to coat the back of a wooden spoon. Do not let it boil or the custard will split. Strain into a clean bowl, lay plastic wrap on the surface to prevent a skin forming and refrigerate for up to 2 days.

MAYONNAISE & VINAIGRETTE

MAYONNAISE
MAKES 500 ML (17 FL OZ/2 CUPS)

4 egg yolks

½ teaspoon white wine vinegar

1 teaspoon lemon juice

500 ml (17 fl oz/2 cups) peanut oil

VINAIGRETTE
MAKES 125 ML (4 FL OZ/½ CUP)

1 garlic clove, crushed

½ teaspoon dijon mustard

1½ tablespoons white wine vinegar

80 ml (3 fl oz/⅓ cup) olive oil

1 For the mayonnaise, put the egg yolks, vinegar and lemon juice in a bowl or food processor and whisk or mix until light and creamy. Add the oil, drop by drop from the tip of a teaspoon, mixing constantly until the mixture begins to thicken, then add the oil in a very thin stream. (If you're using a processor, pour in the oil in a thin stream with the motor running.) Season well.

2 For the vinaigrette, combine the garlic, mustard and vinegar. Add the oil in a thin stream, whisking continuously to form an emulsion. Season with salt and pepper. Store in a screw-top jar in the fridge and shake well before use. You can also add some chopped herbs such as chives or chervil.

BÉCHAMEL SAUCE & VELOUTÉ SAUCE

BÉCHAMEL SAUCE
MAKES 750 ML (27 FL OZ/3 CUPS)

100 g 4 oz) butter

1 onion, finely chopped

90 g (3 oz/¾ cup) plain (all-purpose) flour

1 litre (35 fl oz/4 cups) milk

pinch of nutmeg

bouquet garni

VELOUTÉ SAUCE
MAKES 500 ML (17 FL OZ/2 CUPS)

70 g (2 oz) butter

80 g (3 oz/⅔ cup) plain (all-purpose) flour

1 litre (35 fl oz/4 cups) hot chicken stock

1 For the béchamel sauce, melt the butter in a saucepan, add the onion and cook, stirring, for 3 minutes. Stir in the flour to make a roux and cook, stirring, for 3 minutes over low heat without allowing the roux to brown.

2 Remove from heat and add the milk gradually, stirring after each addition until smooth. Return to the heat, add the nutmeg and bouquet garni and cook for 5 minutes. Strain through a fine sieve into a clean pan and lay a buttered piece of baking paper on the surface to prevent a skin forming.

3 For the velouté sauce, melt butter in a saucepan. Stir in the flour to make a roux and cook, stirring, for 3 minutes over low heat without allowing the roux to brown. Cool to room temperature. Add the hot stock and mix well. Return to the heat and simmer very gently for 10 minutes or until thick. Strain through a fine sieve, cover and refrigerate until needed.

INDEX

A

aïoli — 11
aligot — 115
almonds
    almond pastry — 130
    pithiviers — 129
    tuiles — 142
anchovies
    pan bagnet — 42
    pissaladière — 26
apples
    apple tart — 134
    apples and pears in pastry — 138
    the perfect tarte tatin — 139
    pork chops with Calvados — 82
    poulet Vallée d'Auge — 89
    tourte de blettes — 40
artichokes
    artichokes vinaigrette — 15
    asparagus and artichoke quiche — 36
    lamb and artichoke fricassée — 86
    asparagus and artichoke quiche — 36
asparagus with hollandaise sauce — 14

B

beans
    cassoulet — 77
    lamb braised with beans — 63
    soupe au pistou — 20
béchamel sauce — 157
beef
    beef carbonnade — 62
    beef Provençale — 87
    beef and red wine pies — 43
    biftek haché — 81
    boeuf á la ficelle — 50
    boeuf bourguignon — 79
    boeuf en croute — 67
    boeuf en daube — 64
    entrecôte à la bordelaise — 68
    pot au feu — 83
    steak au poivre — 65
    steak béarnaise — 66
berries
    mixed berry tartlets — 137
    raspberry soufflé — 141
    strawberry millefeuille — 140
    vanilla soufflé with raspberry coulis — 123
biftek haché — 81
blanquette de veau — 70
blue cheese soufflé — 45
boeuf á la ficelle — 50
boeuf bourguignon — 79
boeuf en croute — 67
boeuf en daube — 64
boulangère potatoes — 103
bread
    frisée and garlic crouton salad — 97
    pan bagnet — 42
    pissaladière — 26
    salade Lyonnaise — 96
    bread dough — 149
    brioche — 148

C

cabbage
    cabbage soup — 23
    pork chops with braised red cabbage — 54
cakes
    chocolate-hazelnut cake — 133
    madeleines — 143
capsicums
    piperade — 32
scaramel ice cream — 145
cassoulet — 77
cauliflower soup — 21
celeriac remoulade — 113
cheese
    aligot — 115
    blue cheese soufflé — 45
    croque monsieur — 31
    goat's cheese galette — 41
    gratin dauphinois — 108
    salad with chèvres — 93
    tarte flambée — 27
cherry clafoutis — 128
chicken
    chicken and bacon gougère — 88
    chicken chasseur — 53
    chicken consommé — 17
    chicken with forty cloves of garlic — 51
    chicken liver pâté — 12
    coq au vin — 52
    poule au pot — 80
    poulet Vallée d'Auge — 89
    roast chicken — 57
    tarragon chicken — 55
chocolate mousse — 121
chocolate soufflés — 125
chocolate-hazelnut cake — 133
choux pastry — 153
cinnamon bavarois — 122
coffee crémets with chocolate sauce — 118
coq au vin — 52
courgette soufflé — 44
courgettes see zucchini
couscous, lamb stuffed with couscous and almonds — 76
crème Anglaise — 155
crème brûlée — 124
crème caramel — 126
crème patissière — 155
crêpes — 154
    crêpes suzette — 127
    ham, mushroom and cheese crêpes — 28
croque monsieur — 31

D

desserts
    apple tart — 134
    apples and pears in pastry — 138
    cherry clafoutis — 128
    chocolate mousse — 121
    chocolate soufflés — 125
    cinnamon bavarois — 122
    coffee crémets with chocolate sauce — 118
    crème brûlée — 124
    crème caramel — 126
    crêpes suzette — 127
    gâteau Basque — 130
    île flottante — 131
    lemon tart — 135
    mixed berry tartlets — 137
    peaches cardinal — 144
    pear and almond tart — 136
    pears in red wine — 119
    petits pots de crème — 120
    raspberry soufflé — 141
    strawberry millefeuille — 140
    vanilla soufflé with raspberry coulis — 123
dips
    aïoli — 11
    tapenade — 10
dressings
    mustard mayonnaise — 113
    vinaigrette — 156

E

eggplant, ratatouille tarts — 39
eggs
    asparagus and artichoke quiche — 36
    piperade — 32
    quiche Lorraine — 35
    salade Niçoise — 95
    see also omelettes
entrecôte à la bordelaise — 68

F

fennel
    baked trout with fennel and capers — 60
    fennel, tomato and garlic gratin — 106
    roasted fennel and orange salad — 92
fish cooked in paper — 84
flamiche — 34
French onion soup — 16
fricassée, lamb and artichoke — 86
frisée and garlic crouton salad — 97

G

garlic
  aïoli 11
  chicken with forty cloves of garlic 51
  fennel, tomato and garlic gratin 106
frisée and garlic crouton salad 97
garlic prawns 46
garlic soup 22
gasconnade 78
gasconnade 78
gâteau Basque 130
goat's cheese galette 41
gratin
  fennel, tomato and garlic gratin 106
  gratin dauphinois 108

H

ham
  croque monsieur 31
  ham, mushroom and cheese crêpes 28
hollandaise sauce 14

I

ice cream, caramel 145
île flottante 131

L

lamb
  gasconnade 78
  lamb and artichoke fricassée 86
  lamb braised with beans 63
  lamb stuffed with couscous and almonds 76
  navarin à la printanière 75
  rack of lamb with herb crust 58
  roast leg of lamb with spring vegetables 74
leeks
  flamiche 34
  leek and potato soup 18
  leeks à la grecque 111
  rocket, basil and leek quiche 37
  tian de legumes 105
lemon tart 135
lentils
  braised sausages with puy lentils 59
  lentils in red wine 101
  salt pork with lentils 61

M

madeleines 143
mayonnaise 156
mustard mayonnaise 113
meringue, île flottante 131
mushrooms
  boeuf bourguignon 79
  mushrooms à la grecque 112

mushrooms with tarragon and crème fraîche 98
mustard mayonnaise 113

N

navarin à la printanière 75

O

octopus braised in tomato and wine 85
olives, tapenade 10
omelettes
  omelette aux fines herbes 29
  zucchini omelette 30
onions
  French onion soup 16
  onion tart 33
  peas with onions and lettuce 99
  pissaladière 26
  tarte flambée 27
  vol-au-vents 38

P

pan bagnet 42
Paris-Brest 132
pastry
  beef and red wine pies 43
  boeuf en croute 67
  chicken and bacon gougère 88
  flamiche 34
  gâteau Basque 130
  goat's cheese galette 41
  onion tart 33
  Paris-Brest 132
  Provençal tart 25
  quiche Lorraine 35
  ratatouille tarts 39
  vol-au-vents 38
pastry basics
  choux pastry 153
  puff pastry 152
  sweet pastry 151
  tart pastry 150
pâté
  chicken liver 12
  terrine de campagne 13
peaches cardinal 144
pears
  apples and pears in pastry 138
  pear and almond tart 136
  pears in red wine 119
peas with onions and lettuce 99
pepper, steak au poivre 65
petits farcis 24
petits pots de crème 120
pies
  beef and red wine pies 43
  gâteau Basque 130
  tourte de blettes 40

piperade 32
pissaladière 26
pithiviers 129
pork
  cassoulet 77
  pork chops with braised red cabbage 54
  pork chops with Calvados 82
  pork noisettes with prunes 72
  pork with sage and capers 69
  salt pork with lentils 61
  terrine de campagne 13
pot au feu 83
potatoes
  aligot 115
  boulangère potatoes 103
  gratin dauphinois 108
  leek and potato soup 18
  potato salad 114
  potatoes Anna 107
  tian de legumes 105
poule au pot 80
poulet Vallée d'Auge 89
prawns, garlic 46
Provençal tart 25
puff pastry 152

Q

quiches
  asparagus and artichoke quiche 36
  quiche Lorraine 35
  rocket, basil and leek quiche 37

R

ratatouille 104
ratatouille tarts 39
red mullet, grilled, with herb sauce 56
rocket, basil and leek quiche 37

S

salads
  frisée and garlic crouton salad 97
  potato salad 114
  roasted fennel and orange salad 92
  salad with chèvre 93
  salade Lyonnaise 96
  salade Niçoise 95
  salade with walnuts 94
salt pork with lentils 61
sauces
  béchamel sauce 157
  hollandaise sauce 14
  sauce bordelaise 68
  velouté sauce 157
sausages, braised, with puy lentils 59
scallops Provençale 47
seafood
  baked trout with fennel and capers 60

INDEX

fish cooked in paper	84
garlic prawns	46
grilled red mullet with herb sauce	56
octopus braised in tomato and wine	85
scallops Provençale	47
silverbeet, tourte de blettes	40
soufflés	
blue cheese soufflé	45
chocolate soufflés	125
courgette soufflé	44
raspberry soufflé	141
vanilla soufflé with raspberry coulis	123
soup	
cabbage soup	23
cauliflower soup	21
chicken consommé	17
French onion soup	16
garlic soup	22
leek and potato soup	18
soupe au pistou	20
watercress soup	19
spinach	
purée of spinach	102
roast veal stuffed with ham and spinach	71
starters	
aïoli	11
artichokes vinaigrette	15
chicken liver pâté	12
garlic prawns	46
ham, mushroom and cheese crêpes	28
petits farcis	24
ratatouille tarts	39
scallops Provençale	47
tapenade	10
tarte flambée	27
terrine de campagne	13
vol-au-vents	38
see also soup	
steak au poivre	65
steak béarnaise	66
strawberry millefeuille	140
sweet pastry	151

T

tapenade	10
tarragon chicken	55
tarragon and lemon crème fraîche	98
tart pastry	150
tarte flambée	27
tarte tatin, the perfect	139
tarts	
apple tart	134
chicken and bacon gougère	88
flamiche	34
goat's cheese galette	41
lemon tart	135
mixed berry tartlets	137
onion tart	33
pear and almond tart	136
the perfect tarte tatin	139
Provençal tart	25
ratatouille tarts	39
tarte flambée	27
see also quiches	
terrine de campagne	13
tian of potatoes	105
tomatoes	
octopus braised in tomato and wine	85
petits farcis	24
Provençal tart	25
vegetable tian	110
tourte de blettes	40
trout, baked, with fennel and capers	60
tuiles	142
tuna	
pan bagnet	42
salade Niçoise	95

V

vanilla soufflé with raspberry coulis	123
veal	
blanquette de veau	70
roast veal stuffed with ham and spinach	71
veal paupiettes	73
vegetable tian	110
velouté sauce	157
Vichy carrots	109
vinaigrette	156
vol-au-vents	38

W

walnuts	
salade with chèvres	93
salade with walnuts	94
watercress soup	19
witlof, braised	100

Z

zucchini	
courgette soufflé	44
ratatouille	104
vegetable tian	110
zucchini omelette	30